Praying With Scripture in the Holy Land

Daily Meditations With the Risen Jesus
Illustrated

Msgr. David E. Rosage
Author of *Discovering Pathways to Prayer*

LIVING FLAME PRESS
BOX 74 LOCUST VALLEY, N.Y. 11560

All scripture quotations are from the New American Bible

Nihil Obstat: Rev. Armand M. Nigro, S.J., Censor Librorum

Imprimatur: Rev. Bernard J. Topel, D.D., Ph.D., Bishop of Spokane

All photos from the Israel Ministry of Tourism

Cover: Robert Manning

Published by Living Flame Press / Locust Valley / New York 11560

Copyright 1977: David E. Rosage

ISBN 0-914544-14-4

Printed in the United States of America.

Introduction

When St. Paul reflected on the plan, the presence and the power of God in our lives, he was so overwhelmed that he exclaimed: "How deep are the riches and the wisdom and the knowledge of God! How inscrutable his judgments, how unsearchable his ways!" (*Romans 11:33*). When we take time to reflect on what God is doing in our day we, too, are prone to cry out with joy: "How magnificent all His ways!"

The Holy Spirit breathes where He wills. In this age of the Spirit, we are experiencing His powerful influence in many areas of our life. In this twilight time of the twentieth century, the Holy Spirit is leading us into deeper and richer dimensions of prayer. In the heart of man today, there is an ever-increasing love and longing for the Word of God. The Holy Spirit is creating in us a greater desire and yearning to know more about God, especially as He reveals Himself in Sacred Scripture.

In the past many of us have had only a casual acquaintance with the Bible. Perhaps our curiosity stirred us to search the Scriptures in order to substantiate a doctrine or to confirm a moral standard for our daily living. Few of us had a strong desire to spend time regularly just listening to what God

3

is saying to us in His Word.

Today the Spirit is touching the heart of man and creating within him a thirst for a more intimate and personal knowledge of God. We can best come to know God for what He is as we listen to what He tells us about Himself in His revealed Word. As we listen to His Word in Sacred Scripture, we immediately discover that He is a loving Father who is concerned about even the most insignificant details of our life. As the Holy Spirit touches our hearts with His divine influence, many of us are learning that the Bible is not merely a symbol of our Christianity nor only a source from which we can support many of our beliefs, but rather that it is a personal message from God Himself to each one of us individually. God communicates Himself to man through His Word.

Good communication is a two-way street. We must speak honestly and sincerely, but we must also learn the more difficult process of listening. In order to reach a viable stage of communication with God, we must listen to what He is saying to us. We must spend considerable time in listening at the very depth of our being. We must trust that the Bible is God's message for us at this very moment and in this given situation.

Praying with Scripture is rapidly becoming one of the more popular methods of prayer. This kind of prayer involves, for the most part, listening and loving. Paul briefly summarizes the purpose and value of praying with Scripture in these words: "All Scripture is inspired of God and is useful for teaching — for reproof, correction, and training in holiness so that the man of God may be fully competent and equipped for every good work" (*II Timothy 3:16-17*).

If praying with Scripture is to bear fruit consistently in our lives, there is need for a guide in the selection of texts from the Bible to be used as a launching pad for our prayer. Random choices do not always serve the needs of the moment. We need a broader and more integrated experience of God's Word, a guide.

This book is such a guide. It differs from others in that we have tried to introduce the weekly prayer suggestions with related events in the life of Jesus. We have tried to integrate our experience of visiting the holy places with what Jesus did or taught in these very places. It is to be hoped that this will create an atmosphere which will be conducive to a better understanding of His Word and to more intimate prayer.

Praying With Scripture in the Holy Land is an attempt to revisit and relive with the gloriously Risen Jesus some of the places and events where He walked and wept, where He taught and touched, where He healed and loved. Reflecting on these places of Jesus' ministry should help us not only to prepare for prayer but also to lead us into a deeper union with Him.

We are not here attempting to turn back the clock some 2,000 years, but rather to relive these events with the Risen Jesus present with us and within us at this point in time. In spirit let us imagine that we are sitting with Jesus today and letting Him review for us what He taught and suffered for our redemption. Meeting Jesus in the Gospel and listening to Him with every fibre of our being is prayer at its depth.

No doubt this is what our Bishops were telling us in the Constitution of the Sacred Liturgy: "He [Jesus] is present in His Word, since it is He Himself who speaks when the Holy Scriptures are read in Church" (par. 7). When Jesus speaks to us how intently we should listen to His every word!

Methodology

In order to pray with Sacred Scripture there are a few suggestions which may assist you in acquiring both an exterior and an interior prayer posture. After a brief introduction of a theme for each week of the year, there is a passage of Sacred Scripture suggested for your daily praying. Only the salient thought of the text suggested for the day is printed after the number of the day of the week. In order to pray it will be necessary to read the passage in its entirety as listed, or even to read a whole chapter as a preparation. For example:

(I) *John 10:1-16* "I am the good shepherd. . . . "

Naturally "(I)" means the first day of your week of prayer. The brief quote "I am the good shepherd . . . " is only a hint of what Jesus is saying in the longer suggested passage of John, chapter 10: verses 1 to 16. You may even wish to read the whole chapter before you begin to pray using only a word, a phrase or a thought found in the text. Here are a few hints:

(1) If you prefer to pray in the morning, it would be well to read the suggested scriptural text slowly and reflectively the evening before; let the words settle into your whole being and become a part of you. This remote preparation is conducive to prayer because the Word of God rests in the subconscious mind and conditions you for a personal meeting with Jesus the next morning. If another time of day is more suitable for your prayer a similar procedure of remote preparation is advisable.

(2) Choose a place and posture for prayer which is relaxing. Take a sufficiently long period of time to settle down and feel relaxed. If you

concentrate on your breathing, you will find it a good means of relaxing.

(3) Be aware of the presence of God. As you breathe rhythmically, pronounce the name of Jesus deep in your heart, not with your lips. This will prove helpful in bringing you into an awareness of His abiding presence.

(4) Take up the Word of God and read it reflectively with frequent pauses to ascertain what message the Lord is trying to convey to you. Let it speak to you, a word, a phrase, an expression at a time. Rest with it. Let it sink into your whole being. Let it find a home in your heart. Imagine yourself enjoying the fragrance and flavor of an elegant wine as you sip it appreciatively.

(5) Pray by listening and responding in love. "Be" for God and let Him "be" for you. Rest in His presence. A lover longs to be in the presence of the one he loves. God loves us and we love Him. Hunger for His presence as you await His personal message for you. Then respond to Him in love and gratitude as the Spirit moves you. Your response can also be a wordless response in awe and reverence.

(6) You will find it rewarding to keep a spiritual journal. The daily entry in your journal is a brief account of the highlight of your hour of prayer. A rereading of your journal from time to time will deepen the experience you enjoyed in prayer. This repetition will be extremely beneficial for your spiritual growth.

Fruits

Who of us can estimate the fruits of our praying with His Word? Only God knows. Prayer is the gift of ourselves to God. What happens in prayer is God's gift to us. Occasionally God may permit us to enjoy a very real sense of His presence in prayer. He may even let us see and experience some of the fruits of our own prayer. At other times our prayer may seem dry and fruitless. Let us not be deceived! God is moulding and transforming us even though we may not be aware of His operation within us. Here are some of the fruits of praying with Scripture.

In the first place, we will find renewed inspiration and purpose in our daily routine duties. All of us need this type of motivation constantly.

Secondly, a conversion process will be taking place within us, sometimes without our even being aware of it. Jesus assures us: "You are clean already, thanks to the word I have spoken to you" (*John 15:3*). When we expose our thinking to God's Word, we will recognize the deviations and the tangents which draw us away from the life-style to which He is calling us. We will also discover that our interest in many things will wane while God's will of preference will reach a new priority in our lives.

Thirdly, a great transformation will gradually be effected within us. God's Word has the power to transform us totally. Paul gives us this assurance when he encourages us to: " . . . acquire a fresh, spiritual way of thinking. You must put on that new man created in God's image, whose justice and holiness are born of truth" (*Ephesians 4:23-24*). This is praying by listening to different ways of thinking and also putting on "the new man." Gradually our attitude, our thinking, our reaction to the events of daily living will be radically changed. This is what St. Paul meant when he said: "Your attitude must be that of Christ" (*Philippians 2:5*). As we continue to pray with His Word an even greater (more startling) fruit will accrue to us. Paul assures us: "All of us, gazing on the Lord's glory with unveiled faces, are being transformed from glory to glory into his very image by the Lord who is the Spirit" (*II Corinthians 3:18*).

Finally His Word will bring a peace and joy into our lives which nothing in this world can produce. Jesus explains: "All this I tell you that my joy may be yours and your joy may be complete" (*John 15:11*).

With God's divine favor and blessing may these pages draw us, His adopted sons and daughters, into a deeper relationship with our loving Abba. Through our praying with His Word may the presence and power of the Risen Jesus with us and within us become more and more interiorized and actualized in our lives. Then we can better understand and experience His benevolence: "My peace is my gift to you" (*John 14:27*).

Table of Contents

1. Jesus Bids Us Listen

"Lord, teach us to pray . . . " (Luke 11:1).

On a bright, cheery, toasty warm spring morning we walked through the Garden of Gethsemane up to the top of the Mount of Olives. Our destination was the Pater Noster Shrine. On the top of the Mount of Olives, before one begins the descent down the eastern slope to the village of Bethany, is a shrine which commemorates the site where Jesus was accustomed to spend time in prayer.

Luke relates the fact that one day Jesus was praying here with His disciples. They were captivated by the change in His appearance and manner as He communicated with His Father. His peaceful, joyous countenance radiated an appearance of otherworldliness. This experience moved the disciples to ask, "Lord, teach us to pray." It was then that He taught them the Lord's Prayer (*Luke 11:1ff*). For an obvious reason this is called the Pater Noster Shrine.

Our purpose in going to this shrine was to spend some time in private prayer and also to culminate our personal prayer with the celebration of the Holy Eucharist in a beautiful open-air chapel. The Carmelites, who live in a cloistered convent here, care for the shrine. Some years ago a church was begun on this site but never completed. The raised sanctuary, made of native stone, and the walls about six feet high make this an ideal secluded place of prayer.

After visiting the cave in which Jesus taught the Our Father to the disciples, we found a comfortable place under various trees or in the shade of the wall where we could be alone to pray. I followed the example of the disciples and begged Jesus to teach me how to pray. A new thought came to mind as I sat in the shade of a palm tree. Jesus never really taught His apostles to pray vocally until they asked Him. The reason for this finally dawned upon me. They were already deeply involved in a different type of prayer. Up until this time, and for that matter for the rest of His earthly sojourn, Jesus was teaching them to pray with His Word. He wanted them to ponder and reflect on the Good News He was teaching them.

As they spent time in meditating upon His Word, they were praying. That is why He frequently took them into an olive grove, a desert place or up a mountain to pray. He wanted them to permit His Word to find a home in their hearts. This kind of prayer was radically moulding and transforming their lives without their even being aware of its power. Did He not tell us about the power of His Word when He said: "You are clean already thanks to the word I have spoken to you," and a few verses later: "All this I tell you that my joy may be yours and that your joy may be complete" (*John 15:3, 11*). Only as we pray the Word of God will we understand His will and in that will find true peace and joy. On another occasion Jesus again emphasized the value of praying with His Word: " . . . blest are they who hear the word of God and keep it" (*Luke 11:28*).

As we take up His Word each day as found in the Bible, not simply to read it for information nor out of curiosity, but to ponder and reflect upon that Word, we, like the apostles, will be gradually transformed.

How frequently in Sacred Scripture we are advised to listen. At the transfiguration the Father was quite imperative when He confirmed His Son's mission: "Listen to him." Jesus also admonished His disciples and us: "Whoever is of God hears every word God speaks." The Holy Spirit, too, urges us: "Let him who has ears heed the Spirit's word to the Churches."

Visiting the many areas where Jesus taught and prayed made His Word really come alive for us. We could almost hear Him speak as we read the Gospel message. That same Jesus is abiding with us in His Risen Life. He is speaking to us and inviting us to come apart daily to listen to what He wants to tell us.

The suggested passages from Sacred Scripture will establish a theme for each week. We suggest you use only one text each day for your prayer time. That will draw you more deeply into the message that Jesus wants to impart to you. It is imperative that you listen.

Matthew 17:1-8 — *"This is my beloved Son on whom my favor rests. Listen to him."*

Luke 11:27-28 — *"... blest are they who hear the word of God and keep it."*

John 14:23-26 — *"Anyone who loves me will be true to my word, and my Father will love him; we will come to him and make our dwelling place with him."*

John 8:31-51 — "Whoever is of God hears every word God speaks."

Matthew 13:4-23 — "Let everyone heed what he hears!"

John 6:60-69 — "You have the words of eternal life."

John 12:44-50 — "If anyone hears my words and does not keep them . . . "

2. Sinai — Lure of the Desert

"He lived in the desert until the day when he made his public appearance in Israel" (Luke 1:80).

Early in the morning we left Jerusalem in a nine-passenger plane with Mount Sinai as our destination. The flight down the peninsula was over the bleak, barren and desolate Negev desert to the tip of the Sinai Peninsula. From the air there was no sign of plant, animal or human life in the desert. All we could see was rock and sand, mountainous peaks of rocks and endless valleys of sand. Our landing strip was a short, narrow, paved runway in the midst of this desert of sand and rocks.

We bade farewell to our pilot and boarded a large, four-wheel-drive truck which took us some

Masada — the remote last stronghold of the Jewish rebels against Rome.

20 miles over sand-strewn roads to the base of Mount Sinai. We discovered that there is not a single stream in the entire peninsula which flows into the sea. Here we experienced the desert in closer contact. Again we were surrounded by sand and rocks. The wind caused the sand to shift constantly.

We did see a few Bedouin families living here and there. Wherever there is any supply of water from a spring or well, there is sure to be some sign of life. These Bedouins live in tents made of camel and goat skins. A few goats and chickens are their only possessions.

After a rough, dusty ride in the open truck we came to the Monastery of St. Catherine situated at the base of Mount Musa, which is another name for Mount Sinai. It is also called Mount Horeb in the Scriptures.

Here in this canyon of rock Justinian built a monastery in the sixth century. At first it was dedicated to our Blessed Mother. Later, according to legend, the bones of St. Catherine were carried here by angels. Since then it has been called St. Catherine's. Here we find possibly the greatest collection of icons, including the second oldest one in the world. The library is the oldest in the world and contains some 6,000 volumes in 12 different languages. Here was found the *Codes Sinaiticus*, a Greek translation of the Bible dating from the third century. About a dozen Greek Orthodox monks live here. A young monk who spoke English gave us a tour of some of the areas which many visitors never see. The monks treasure their solitude immensely. Here also is the site of the burning bush where God spoke to Moses and directed him to free His people from Egypt.

The lure of the desert, the challenge it presents, the nothingness it offers, the threat even to one's survival, all this must be a real, live experience in order to draw one close to God. Men of all times have been drawn to the desert to find that solitude and silence which is so essential to prayer.

Jesus, too, retired to the desert to be alone with His Father. He invites us into the desert of our own heart. He wishes us to seek the desert of solitude and prayer often so that we can become genuinely aware of our own nothingness, our total and absolute dependence upon Him.

We need not go off to some distant desert for this soul-searching. In a certain sense Jesus fulfills in His person all that we seek in a desert. He is the living water, the bread from heaven, the way and the guide, the light in the night, the serpent who gives life to all who look on it to be saved. He is the one in whom we find the ultimate knowledge of the Father by sharing His flesh and blood. In Him we can overcome all sorts of trials. In Him we have perfect communion with God. Hence we can say that the desert as place and time is fulfilled in Jesus.

Try to live this desert experience with Him as you pray.

Exodus 3:1-17 — *"Remove the sandals from your feet, for the place where you stand is holy ground."*

Deuteronomy 8:1-15 — *"Remember how for forty years now the Lord, your God, has directed all your journeying in the desert. . . . "*

Matthew 4:1-11 — *"Then Jesus was led into the desert by the Spirit. . . . "*

Hosea 2:16-25 — *"I will lead her into the desert and speak to her heart."*

19

Mark 1:32-35 — ". . . he went off to a lonely place in the desert. . . ."

Psalm 78:1-31 — "He made streams flow from the crag and brought the waters forth in rivers."

Mark 6:30-32 — "Come by yourselves to an out-of-the-way place and rest a little."

3. Sinai — A Challenging Climb

". . . the tops of the mountains are his" (Psalm 95:4).

Mount Sinai rises majestically in the bright desert sun. It has a built-in attraction about it. It challenges one to want to climb to its summit. However, the sacredness of God's presence on that mountain has an even greater lure.

After our visit to the monks in St. Catherine's Monastery we drove around to the other side of the mountain. There we found a narrow pathway threading its way around imposing cliffs and large boulders. This pathway leads onward and always upward. Sometimes it was gradual, sometimes quite steep. At times we even came upon some steps on our three-and-one-half hour climb to the top. These steps were large rocks placed there by the monks many years ago. In fact, one monk was supposed to have spent 50 years working on this stairway. Sometimes the treads on this rock stairway were a convenient eight-inch rise, another time two or three feet to be scaled.

As we began our precipitous and somewhat dangerous ascent we agreed to make it in silence so that we could better experience some of the thrill and awe with which Moses approached the summit of this peak. As we climbed higher and higher we were gradually leaving the surrounding peaks below us. I was beginning to understand why it took Moses 40 days and 40 nights on the mountain. I am sure that much of the time was consumed in climbing.

When God brought the Israelites into this area after their release from the slavery of Egypt, He wanted them to realize that He, alone, was their God and that they could not possibly survive without His providential care and concern. The desert taught them that lesson well. Here was no water, no food, no security — nothing but sand and mountains of rock. The desert can become stiflingly hot by day and cold at night. Without God's loving providence this motley group of freed slaves could not possibly have survived. This was truly a testing ground.

How glibly I had often described the situation of the Israelites being brought by God into the desert where they could really be made aware of their utter dependence upon God. Often I had spoken about the poverty of spirit which this environment helped them to cultivate. However, I had to go into that desert to experience what the desert says to us. I had to taste the sand in my mouth, feel it in my ears and shoes. I had to feel the burning sun by day and the bitter chill of the wind at night. I had to experience the absolute nothingness. I had to commune with God because there was nothing and no one else. There was absolutely nothing other than the presence of God. It was a personal experience I shall never forget.

Back in the third century a monk wrote that he

walked 18 days into the desert to pray. After he had spent considerable time in prayer, he decided to remain in the desert where he had found God. He, and the other hermits after him, lived alone in caves and there communed with God. This was the beginning of a new style of life. Eventually these hermits began to form little communities. This was the beginning of monastic life in this remote desert.

After my personal experience of helplessness in the Sinai Desert, I was beginning to understand more fully my own creaturehood as totally dependent upon a loving Abba-Father.

The desert is God's House of Prayer. The monks in Sinai and those all over the world have been lured into the desert to find God. We hope that praying His Word during these next few days will draw us into that prayer-posture of total dependence on Him.

Deuteronomy 5:6-10 — "*I, the Lord, am your God. . . .*"

John 15:1-8 — "*. . . apart from me you can do nothing.*"

Psalm 106:1-48 — "*Give thanks to the Lord, for he is good.*"

Isaiah 40:12-17 — "*Who . . . weighed the mountains in scales and the hills in a balance?*"

Hebrews 3:12-19 — "*. . . it was their unbelief that kept them from entering.*"

Isaiah 43:19-22 — "*For I put water in the desert and rivers in the wasteland . . .*"

Isaiah 35:1-10 — "The desert and the parched land will exult. . . . "

4. Sinai's Singular Summit

*" . . . the mountain God has chosen
for his throne, where the Lord himself
will dwell forever?" (Psalm 68:17).*

It was a tedious climb, but at long last we reached the summit of Mount Sinai, rising majestically 7,362 feet above sea level and 2,349 feet above St. Catherine's Monastery. From this vantage point all the other peaks seemed dwarfed below us. As I gazed at the breathtaking view all around us the words of the psalmist rang in my heart: "The tops of the mountains are his" (*Psalm 95:4*). This is the very spot where Moses met God face to face. Here, God was very present to me. The bleakness of the desert far below spoke to me of our dire need for God's loving providence in our lives.

As we gazed in wonder at the mountains below us we could see black streaks, called dykes, like huge strata cutting through the mountains. This was some of the molten rock pushed to the surface by the eruptions occurring in the earth, and was apparent in many parts of the desert. Turquoise was also found in these black mountains. The desert holds many secrets.

At the very peak of the mountain we found the cave where Elijah sought refuge from the wrath of Jezebel (*I Kings 19:1ff*). A small chapel is built over the cave. Here we offered the Holy Sacrifice of the Mass. It was my privilege to be the principal celebrant. It was a moving experience because like Moses, and later, Elijah, I felt the presence of God hovering over us.

After Mass we enjoyed our sack lunch together, then went off to spend some time in prayer. Many thoughts raced through my mind. I thought of Moses climbing up this mountain on which God had written the decalogue. It was here also that God revealed His name to Moses. After Moses had broken the tablets, God again wrote His Law on the stone which Moses had prepared and brought to the top of the mountain.

Sinai was only the temporary meeting place of God with His people. He is the transcendent God of heaven and earth, but He is also an immanent God who wants to be with His people.

As the Israelites were beginning to comprehend the transcendence of God, He wanted to move more intimately among them. It was at this time that God instructed Moses to build the Tent of Meeting, where God manifested His presence by means of a cloud by day and a pillar of fire by night. This was called the *Shekinah (Deuteronomy 12:11; 14:23; 16:2)*.

Truly this is a sacred spot — far removed from all that is mundane. The solitary experience on this mountain, the sheer drop over the many precipices, the gentle breeze which manifested God's presence to Elijah — all made God's presence very real to me.

God invites all of us into a desert experience. It may be a retreat away from the world in one of the many retreat houses throughout our country. It may be a private retreat, a poustinia experience, solitude in our own room or time spent in some hallowed place of prayer. We are so busy that often it is only in the solitude of our own heart that God can reach us. That is why God tells us through His prophet Hosea: "I will lead her into the desert and speak to her heart" (*Hosea 2:16*).

God does not necessarily expect us to seek out a desert area far removed from home. Each one of us can find a desert right in our own environment where we can be alone with God and where He can speak to our heart. Perhaps these suggested scriptural texts will help us enter into a desert experience.

Exodus 15:22-27 — *"What are we to drink?"*

Exodus 16:1-15 — *"I will now rain down bread from heaven for you."*

Deuteronomy 32:1-14 — *"So he spread his wings to receive them and bore them up on his pinions."*

Exodus 19:1-25 — *"... I bore you up on eagle wings and brought you here to myself."*

I Kings 19:1-14 — *"... the Lord will be passing by."*

Exodus 34:1-9 — *"Get ready for tomorrow morning, when you are to go up Mount Sinai and there present yourself to me on the top of the mountain."*

Acts 7:30-50 — *"... it was he [Moses] who was in conversation with the angel on Mount Sinai. ..."*

5. Sinai — Wandering Through a Wadi

"Even though I walk in the dark valley
I fear no evil;
for you are at my side . . . " (Psalm 23:4).

There is still another aspect of our Sinai expedition which spoke volumes to me. We descended Mount Sinai by another route. It was shorter, but far more dangerous, especially since we were tired and our footing less secure. God certainly had His arms around each one of us.

When we reached the base of our mountain we found the truck waiting for us. Soon we were on our way to a little town called Dahab on the Gulf of Elat. As we proceeded east the sun was just beginning to set. Our journey of some 60 miles was through a dry riverbed called a wadi. The roadway at best was a few tracks in the sand where other vehicles had travelled. As we bounced and bumped along, we had no assurance that a huge rock might not have rolled into our pathway, nor that the wind had not drifted a huge pile of sand in our way. It was quite dark now and the huge mountains of rock hemmed us in on both sides. In the dark they stood out like huge fortresses towering over us. As we journeyed along, a few small desert plants loomed up in the dark shadows. Our imaginations could conjure up many weird forms and shapes.

Here and there we discovered an occasional acacia tree. God instructed Moses to use the wood of this tree to build the Ark of the Covenant. This tree is a desert plant and is hardly more than a bush, reaching a height of six to eight feet. To me the acacia tree is sacred because it had been singled out by God for this special purpose.

It was getting quite cold and wind penetrated to the very marrow of our bones in the open-air truck. We covered ourselves with everything available, even pieces of plastic.

This wadi was probably the very route which the Israelites had taken as they went east before turning north to the Promised Land. As we rumbled along, it was such a thrill to be travelling the very ground which the Israelites crossed so many centuries ago. I was grateful to God for all that has transpired in salvation history and for all those people who have played a role in bringing the faith to me.

Our journey through the wadi was fraught with many dangers. It is not uncommon for vehicles to break down because of the rough terrain. A mountain slide could easily have trapped us and blocked our way. We could have been bogged down in the shifting sand. Yes, many things could have happened, but our loving Father had sent His angels to guide and protect us.

This journey through the wadi reminded me of our pilgrimage through life. Danger is always imminent. There are so many influences crowding in upon us to wean us away from God, our final destiny at our journey's end. We can get mired down so easily in the sand of the mundane and unimportant tasks which obscure our vision, causing us to lose sight of our primary priority. Thus we have less and less time for God. The evil one with all his subtle allurements towers over us at all times, eager to divert us from our God-given mission in life.

It took us long hours to make the trip to Dahab. The Lord used these hours to impress upon me the implications inherent in my own journey through life back to the Father. I am deeply grateful for that experience.

Together let us reflect on the message He has for

each one of us as we listen to His Word.

Deuteronomy 8:6-20 — "For the Lord, your God, is bringing you into a good country. . . . "

I Corinthians 10:1-13 — "He will not let you be tested beyond your strength."

Deuteronomy 1:6-8 — "Go now and occupy the land I swore to your fathers. . . . "

Psalm 81:1-17 — "In distress you called, and I rescued you. . . . "

Exodus 13:21-23 — "Neither the column of cloud by day nor the column of fire by night ever left its place in front of the people."

Isaiah 40:1-5 — "Make straight in the wasteland a highway for our God!"

John 14:16-18 — "I will not leave you orphaned. . . . "

Herodion, Judea — the fortress in the desert built by Herod.

6. The Devil and the Desert

"You are my rock and my fortress;
for your name's sake
you will lead and guide me" (Psalm 31:4).

After a restful night spent in a modern motel on the shore of the Gulf of Elat and an early morning swim in the refreshing waters of the sea, we began the long journey by bus of some 400 miles back to Jerusalem. Our route took us directly north through the Sinai Desert, into the wastelands of the Negev, on to the desolate country around the Dead Sea and the desert area of the Judean hills, and past the Mount of Temptations into Jerusalem.

It was a long, arduous day, but we welcomed the time to reflect on the country through which we were travelling and also on the happenings of the previous day. As I recalled the events of salvation history which had taken place in this land, the presence of God became very real to me. Yes, the desert was speaking to me.

Our route took us over some of the same terrain which Moses and the Israelites had walked on their way to the Promised Land. Because of some powerful, but unfriendly, tribes living to the north, Moses turned east and then north to Mount Nebo from which he viewed the Promised Land. Later Joshua led the Israelites into the Promised Land near Jericho.

Along our route we stopped at King Solomon's mines where copper was obtained for its manifold uses even in those ancient times. We visited the Coral World at Eilat along the Gulf of Elat or Aqaba. In all my life I have never seen fish so exquisitely beautiful and in such a variety of rich colors. All of them are native to these waters. This coral paradise is a favorite haven for scuba divers.

Our brief stopover in the underwater observatory and aquarium spoke very clearly to me of the infinite beauty of God's creation.

Our next stop was Avdat where we offered Mass in the ruins of an old Byzantine basilica built here in the area of the Nabateans. These early people, even in the time of Jesus, had solved their water problem by bringing water into their land by means of aqueducts. Their land was fertile and productive.

As we approached the Dead Sea, sometimes called the Salt Sea, the site of the town of Sodom was pointed out to us. We also saw several pillars, one of which is considered to be Lot's wife, who was turned into a pillar of salt (*Genesis 19:26*).

From the highway we could see the Mount of Temptations. This flat-top mountain is reputed to be the mountain where Jesus took refuge when He "was led into the desert by the Spirit to be tempted by the devil" (*Matthew 4:1ff*).

As it was growing dark and visibility was poor, I could more easily reflect on the desert and the temptations of Jesus. If we can more easily find God in the desert, we can also be assured that Satan will be there with all his intrigue. This was the case with Jesus when He went into the desert to be alone with His Father. At that very time and place He was bombarded by the evil one. The devil used every ruse, especially couching his allurements in the language of Scripture, to divert Jesus from fulfilling what the Father had asked of Him.

Jesus wished to live again the episodes and experiences of the Israelites in the desert. As were the chosen people, Jesus was led into the desert to be tested.

Unlike His forefathers, He overcame the temptations and trials and remained faithful to God. Jesus preferred the Word of God to bread. Thus He replied to the tempter: "Not on bread alone is man to live." Jesus also was willing to trust rather than depend on a striking miracle; hence His reply: "You shall not put the Lord your God to the test." Finally, Jesus preferred to serve God alone rather than hope for any earthly kingdom. "You shall do homage to the Lord your God; him alone shall you adore."

Let us find inspiration and strength in the Word of the Lord as He speaks to us.

Luke 4:1-13 — "You shall not put the Lord your God to the test."

Matthew 26:36-46 — "Be on guard, and pray that you may not undergo the test."

II Corinthians 12:1-10 — "My grace is enough for you, for in weakness power reaches perfection."

Sirach 2:1-11 — "For in fire gold is tested, and worthy men in the crucible of humiliation."

Deuteronomy 6:16-19 — "You shall not put the Lord, your God, to the test. . . . "

James 1:12-15 — "Happy the man who holds out to the end through trial!"

Matthew 5:10-12 — "Blest are those persecuted for holiness' sake. . . . "

Nazareth — the Church of the Annunciation.

7. Nazareth — Yes, Lord

"I am the servant of the Lord" (Luke 1:38).

When we returned to Nazareth I studied the main entrances of the Basilica of the Annunciation. The entrance on the west called the Facade of the Incarnation is adorned with the words: "Verbum Caro Factum Est." On the east we find the Facade of the Virgin Mary adorned with the words of the Salve Regina.

Nazareth is not mentioned in the Old Testament. It seems that God wanted to reserve it exclusively for the great mystery of the Incarnation. He did not want this message to be distorted by any previous history. The name means "flower" or "blossom." What a fitting name for this place where Incarnate Life blossomed forth.

We were privileged to offer the Holy Sacrifice of the Mass in the lower crypt, beside the grotto built over part of the house where Our Lady lived when the Archangel Gabriel appeared to her. I had the experience of sitting outside Mary's door to spend some time in preparation for Mass. As I sat there I pondered the momentous decision which was made on this spot. I listened with my heart as I read St. Luke's account of what took place in this humble abode. My heartbeat quickened when I heard again the total, unconditional commitment which Mary made to God. Her response touched the very core of my being. Here was the actual spot where the Angel Gabriel asked Mary to become the Mother of God. Even though Mary had no previous warning, she immediately and without reservation gave herself to God.

I could almost hear her words: "I am the servant of the Lord. Let it be done to me as you say" (*Luke 1:38*). Each time I have prayed the Hail

Mary or the Angelus since that day, the words have taken on a greater and deeper significance.

These words gave me reason to pause and reflect on my own personal commitment to my Father. God calls each one of us to a special vocation and a particular mission in life. As I pondered Mary's words, an awareness of my lack of generosity in responding to God surfaced. I thought, too, how often my self-concern, my desire for some sort of reassurance, my indolence prevents me from saying "Yes" to the Father as I go about my daily routine duties.

I could see myself more clearly as I pondered Mary's unconditional "Yes" to God. My conscience began to prick me. I realized, too, that the Holy Spirit does not accuse us, nor does He cause tension within us unless He also gives us hope and encouragement to deepen our commitment.

That day in Nazareth the Holy Spirit, who had overshadowed Mary so powerfully, taught me again the paradox of giving. He reminded me once again that it is more blessed to give than to receive. We enjoy greater happiness and deeper peace as we give of ourselves unstintingly. Jesus promised that the Holy Spirit "will instruct you in everything and remind you of all that I told you" (*John 14:26*). The Holy Spirit teaches us that the more graciously we are able to say "Yes" to the Father the happier and the holier we will be.

Later on during Mass the principal celebrant paused at the time for the preparation of the gifts and suggested that all of us take time to recommit ourselves to God, to offer ourselves once again at this offertory time, at this same place where Mary uttered her "fiat."

My prayer that day, and since, has been a fervent plea to our Blessed Mother that through her powerful intercession she may obtain for me the strength and generosity I need to comply with the will of the Father as unreservedly and as perseveringly as she did.

Let us pray with Mary as we listen to God's Word.

Luke 1:26-38 – "I am the servant of the Lord."

Judith 15:9-10 – "You are the glory of Jerusalem. . . . "

Luke 1:39-56 – "God who is mighty has done great things for me. . . . "

Acts 9:1-19 – "Get up and go into the city, where you will be told what to do."

John 2:1-11 – "They have no more wine. . . . Do whatever he tells you."

Mark 10:17-27 – "After that, come and follow me."

II Corinthians 1:18-22 – "Jesus Christ . . . was not alternately 'yes' and 'no'; he was never anything but 'yes.'

8. Ain Karem — The Visitation

"Blessed are you, daughter,
by the Most High God,
above all the women on earth . . . " (Judith 13:18).

Ain Karem is the land where Mary sang that joyous hymn of praise, the Magnificat. It is also the land where the Benedictus burst forth from the heart of Zechariah at the cradle of his son.

As we left the Church of St. John, bound for the Church of the Visitation, we passed by a spring called the Fountain of the Virgin. I wanted to drink from this spring, but it had flooded the whole area around so that I would have had to wade through mud and water to get to it.

A short walk up the hill brought us to the beautiful iron gate in front of the Shrine of the Visitation. This marks the spot where Elizabeth met her cousin Mary. On the facade of this building is an attractive mosaic entitled "The Arrival of Mary in Ain Karem." The church is beautifully decorated with frescoes and mosaics recalling many of the events of salvation history, especially those in which our Blessed Mother played a prominent role. It has been called the most artistic church in the Holy Land. Certainly this is a holy place of quiet and beauty where everything speaks of the glorification of Mary. There seems to be a reflective yet festive atmosphere around the entire shrine.

The pavement reproduces the fauna and flora of the earth, sea and sky. The Magnificat is reproduced in 41 languages on the wall facing the entrance of the church.

It was easy to reflect on the meeting of the great personages at this hallowed spot: Mary and Elizabeth, Jesus and John. The joy of that meeting still echoes throughout the world as we pray and sing

Mary's sublime canticle, the Magnificat.

As we prayed in this sacred spot three lessons spoke to me. First: Mary's loving solicitude which prompted her to go in haste into the hill country to a town in Judah some 90 miles away from home. Elizabeth needed her during those days of her confinement. Mary did not count the cost, nor did she excuse herself because of her own pregnancy. She went in haste to be of service to Elizabeth.

The second lesson was the joy and exaltation which these two women experienced as they came together to recall what God was doing in their day. How joyously Elizabeth received her young cousin and recognized in her the Mother of her Lord! It could have been otherwise. Elizabeth had suffered disgrace and humiliation for many long years because she was barren. In those days sterility was considered a punishment from God. Now Mary, her young cousin, came, especially favored by God. Humanly speaking there could have been tinges of envy, but no such thought spoiled this meeting because both women were close to God.

This lesson obviously speaks of the joy and praise, the peace and tranquility which should pervade our hearts at all times because of the presence and power of God within us. This joy did surface in our group. As we were praying silently in this beautiful church, one of our priests proceeded to the front of the church, turned toward us and, with his eyes closed, sang the Magnificat joyously and professionally. How Mary's words reverberated in our hearts!

The third lesson is Mary's generous giving of herself without counting the cost. Like her we have many occasions when we might be of service to others. Through her powerful intercession let us ask for this grace to give ourselves as generously and graciously as she gave herself.

As we pray this week with these suggested passages, may our hearts be flooded with that peace and joy which only God can give.

Luke 1:39-56 — "My being proclaims the greatness of the Lord. . . . "

I Samuel 1:28-2:10 — "My heart exults in the Lord, my horn is exalted in my God."

Song of Songs 2:8-17 — "Hark! My lover — here he comes springing across the mountains, leaping across the hills."

Psalm 66:1-20 — "Hear now, all you who fear God, while I declare what he has done for me."

Joel 2:19-27 — "And you shall know that I am in the midst of Israel. . . . "

Luke 11:27-28 — "Rather, . . . blest are they who hear the word of God and keep it."

Psalm 113:1-9 — "He establishes in her home the barren wife as the joyful mother of children."

9. Ain Karem — St. John in the Mountains

"In the desert prepare the way
of the Lord! Make straight in the wasteland
a highway for our God!" (Isaiah 40:3).

Ain Karem is an attractive village surrounded by olive trees and vineyards. Its name means "vineyard spring." The name of this village dates back to the Bronze Age. It is mentioned twice in the Old Testament (*Joshua 15:59* and *Jeremiah 6:1*). The fame of this village rests on the historical fact that it was the homeland of John the Baptist. From the time of the Middle Ages it has been known as St. John in the Mountains.

Two great events of salvation history took place here: the meeting of Mary and her cousin Elizabeth, and the birth of John the Baptist. The Church of St. John the Baptist is erected over the place of his birth. The high altar is dedicated to the Baptist, while the altar in the nave on the right is dedicated to his mother, Elizabeth.

When you approach the front of the church, in the nave on the left you will discover a staircase leading down into a grotto. This is venerated as the birthplace of John, and it formed part of the home of Zechariah, John's father.

As we paused to pray in this church, two thoughts dominated my reflection. God's ways are not our ways. God manifested His power and His presence by causing Elizabeth to conceive at an age far beyond that of normal childbearing years. This took place only after the angel announced to Zechariah that his wife, Elizabeth, would conceive and bear a son. Thus God proved that He had a special design on the lives of these people.

Zechariah recognized and rejoiced in that divine

power and presence by uttering the Benedictus, a classic hymn which reverberated throughout the centuries and which is prayed daily throughout the world.

When God is operative in an extraordinary way in the lives of His creatures, He has a specific plan for them. God does nothing purposelessly or simply to be dramatic.

Secondly, I thought of how God had called John to a special vocation. His miraculous birth made this evident to all his relatives. John was the last of the Old Testament or, if you will, the first of the New Testament prophets. He was called to prepare the way of the Lord. "Make ready the way of the Lord" (*Isaiah 40:3* and *Luke 3:4*).

In order to prepare for this mission John spent long years in the desert. This holy youth was eager for silence and solitude so that he could hear the Word of the Lord and prepare himself to announce that Word to his people. He spent his novitiate in a quiet, uninhabited place which, in the New Testament, is usually called a "desert."

This desert was in the neighborhood of his native village. Here he spent a great part of his boyhood preparing himself in austerity for his great mission as precursor of the Messiah. "He lived in the desert until the day when he made his public appearance in Israel" (*Luke 1:80*).

In this biblical event God is teaching us a valuable lesson. Each one of us is called to a particular work in life. In order to keep our minds and hearts attuned to God's will, we must spend time in quiet listening away from the hubbub and the maddening pace of contemporary life. Such moments spent alone with God will be a source of much consolation and reassurance toward our goal in life and will help us to keep our focus on God.

Live the experience of John the Baptist during

41

these next few days. It will bring you much hope and encouragement.

Luke 1:5-24 — *"Your wife Elizabeth shall bear a son whom you shall name John."*

Luke 1:57-66 — *"His name is John."*

Luke 1:67-80 — *"And you, O child, shall be called prophet of the Most High. . . . "*

Luke 3:1-20 — *"Make ready the way of the Lord. . . . "*

Mark 6:14-29 — *"Herod feared John, knowing him to be an upright and holy man. . . . "*

John 3:22-30 — *"He must increase, while I must decrease."*

Isaiah 40:1-5 — *"Comfort, give comfort to my people. . . . "*

Bethlehem — the churches and spires of Christ's birthplace.

10. Shepherds' Field — Bethlehem

"And you, Bethlehem, land of Judah,
are by no means the least
among the princes of Judah . . . " (Matthew 2:6).

Mention the name of Bethlehem and all the joy, the bells and the music of Christmas well up in our souls. The good wishes of peace, joy and merriment of Christmas re-echo in our hearts.

The same spirit of expectation and excitement arose within me as we approached the Shepherds' Field on a beautiful spring morning. The emerald green carpet of spring formed a perfect setting for the countless and varicolored wild flowers blanketing the whole terrain. The terraces of grapevines and olive trees were magnificently decorated with the magic of spring wild flowers. The extravagance of God's creative genius made me pause in awe and reverence.

What an enchanting setting was that place in which the celestial band of angels sang that hymn of praise and glory to God and their reassurance of peace on earth! As my eyes followed the words of their song on the pages of Luke's Gospel, I could almost hear that heavenly chant: "Glory to God in high heaven, peace on earth to those on whom his favor rests" (*Luke 2:14*).

When we arrived the whole terrain was bathed in the brilliant midmorning sunshine of spring. After a rapid survey of the whole area, we paused to spend some time in prayer. I found a shady tree high on the hill from which I could take in the whole landscape. Here I read very slowly and reflectively St. Luke's account of the appearance of the angels to the shepherds. In my mind's eye the shepherds of biblical renown were beginning to come alive again.

From my vantage point I could see a number of shepherds with little flocks of sheep and goats devouring the luscious spring vegetation. These were modern shepherds, but they still wore the traditional dress and followed many of the customs of their ancestors. I am sure that Jesus saw them in the same style of dress.

As I watched these men with their little flocks I could understand why Jesus loved shepherds. They were simple, happy people. Their love and dedication to their sheep was most edifying. Their eyes were ever alert as they kept a keen watch over their flocks. As I watched one shepherd a little lamb came up to him and nudged him gently. The shepherd patted the lamb tenderly and lovingly and it gamboled off with its mother.

After some time spent in prayer we moved into the large cave which often sheltered the shepherds from the cold, wind and rain. Here on a simple but beautiful stone altar we celebrated the Holy Eucharist. It was Christmas all over again. Jesus was present there just as really and truly as He was on the first Christmas night.

How often I have said, "Every day is Christmas because every day Jesus is born again on our altars." The impact of this expression really hit me that morning.

I was pretty much alone with these thoughts when the celebrant invited us to join with him in singing "Glory to God in the Highest." Judging from the response to his invitation and the joy which sprang from so many hearts, I knew that others were being gifted by God with many wonderful experiences of His living presence among us.

Luke 2:8-20 — "The shepherds returned, glorifying and praising God. . . ."

Micah 5:1-4 — "He shall stand firm and shepherd his flock by the strength of the Lord. . . . "

Ruth 1:1-22 — "Your people shall be my people, and your God my God. . . . They went on together till they reached Bethlehem. . . . "

Matthew 2:5-6 — "And you, Bethlehem, . . . are by no means least among the princes of Judah. . . . "

I Samuel 17:12-15 — "David would . . . come from Saul to tend his father's sheep at Bethlehem."

Matthew 2:16-18 — "(Herod) . . . ordered the massacre of all the boys two years old and under in Bethlehem and its environs. . . . "

Ruth 4:1-17 — "May you do well in Ephrathah and win fame in Bethlehem."

11. David's Town of Bethlehem

*"This day in David's City
a savior has been born to you,
the Messiah and Lord" (Luke 2:11).*

When one leaves the hallowed atmosphere of the Shepherds' Field to go to Bethlehem to the spot venerated as the place where Jesus was born, one will, at first, be greatly disappointed. The large basilica over the spot is not comparable to the simple, but beautiful, dome-shaped chapel which the Canadians built in the Shepherds' Field. In order to enter the large basilica one must bend over considerably to pass through the low stone opening in the wall of the church.

The lintel of the opening is a large rock resting horizontally on two equally large boulders placed vertically to form the jamb of the passageway. This type of doorway was built for protection in time of war. Certainly no horse could be ridden into the church.

The place which supposedly marks the spot where Jesus was born and laid in a manger is a crypt beneath the sanctuary of the main portion of the basilica. Several Christian denominations claim a portion of the crypt. A large metal star on the floor beneath one of the altars is marked as the spot where Jesus was born.

However, as I lingered to pray and reflect in this crypt, I was soon oblivious to all the gingerbread decorations and the pilgrims coming and going. Suddenly the hanging sanctuary lights, the faded and dismal draperies, the cold marble floor were unimportant. I became totally unaware of everything about me. As I knelt in this sacred spot tears filled my eyes as St. John's words came to mind: "Yes, God so loved the world that he gave his only Son" (*John 3:16*).

Thanks to St. Francis my mind visualized the Christmas crèche. I was present with Joseph and Mary. I listened as the shepherds came and I heard them leaving praising and glorifying God. I observed as Joseph's watchful, smiling eyes gazed tenderly at Mary. I could also see the awe and reverence on his face as he looked at the infant Jesus. That quiet radiance of Mary's face was indescribable.

Then the impact of my own priesthood struck

me very forcefully. I was reminded of the words of Jesus: "I will not leave you orphaned; I will come back to you" (*John 14:18*). And again: "And know that I am with you always, until the end of the world!" (*Matthew 28:20*). Then the pleading yet imperative words of Jesus spoken to His first priests and all other priests: "Do this as a remembrance of me" (*Luke 22:19*).

Yes, in the Eucharistic Liturgy Jesus is born again. The Holy Sacrifice of the Mass is Bethlehem renewed each day in my life. Bethlehem spoke to me of my personal involvement as a priest in the mystery of the Incarnation. Jesus is born again eucharistically to assure us of His abiding and sustaining presence with us and within us.

As we left that spot I found myself humming over and over again, "O little town of Bethlehem. . . . "

As you pray these suggested scriptural passages this week, may you, too, relive Bethlehem.

Luke 2:1-8 — "She gave birth to her first-born son and wrapped him in swaddling clothes and laid him in a manger. . . . "

Matthew 1:18-25 — " . . . they shall call him Emmanuel. . . . "

John 1:1-16 — "To his own he came, yet his own did not accept him."

Isaiah 7:10-15 — " . . . the virgin shall be with child, and bear a son, and shall name him Emmanuel."

Isaiah 9:1-6 — "For a child is born to us, a son is given us . . . "

John 3:14-16 — "Yes, God so loved the world that he gave his only Son. . . . "

I John 4:7-16 — ". . . he sent his only Son to the world that we might have life through him."

12. Nazareth — Holy Family

"He went down with them then,
and came to Nazareth,
and was obedient to them" (Luke 2:51).

The long sojourn of Jesus in Nazareth makes it a sacred place for all who believe. Here Jesus spent 30 years with Mary and Joseph. This long period of His earthly sojourn is epitomized in a brief statement in Sacred Scripture: "They returned to Galilee and their own town of Nazareth" (*Luke 2:39*).

Nazareth was always important in New Testament history. It was venerated since the earliest Christian times as a precious place. In fact, there is evidence that the relatives of Jesus safeguarded and preserved this spot from the time that Jesus was driven out of His own hometown (*Luke 4*). Nazareth is also the most completely documented of all the sacred places in the Holy Land.

Nazareth is situated in an agricultural area. Perhaps it received its name, Nazareth, meaning "blossom," because of its fertility. Today remains of silos, granaries, cisterns, oil presses and mills tell the story of the past centuries.

At the present time the town is increasing rapidly in population. Nazareth is divided into quarters. Catholics reside in the west and south. Today one finds many Catholic religious communities established in Nazareth.

Nazareth is sacred to us because the Holy Family resided there for such a long period of time. Jesus, Mary and Joseph spent more time in Nazareth than any other place on earth. Here the Holy Family lived in one of the many buildings made of stone. Their home was not isolated on a separate lot as are homes today. Most probably it was a unit in a large complex of homes.

The kind of home in which the Holy Family lived is relatively unimportant. Of much more consequence is the Holy Family itself. Surely there was never a home in which we could find more love, peace, and joy than in that holy dwelling.

A virtue which characterized that home was obedience and willing submission to God and to one another. Joseph proved beyond any shadow of doubt that he was willing to accept whatever God asked of him. He willingly accepted the instructions of the messenger in going to Bethlehem, to Egypt, and back to Galilee. Mary, too, had committed herself without reservation to God's will, regardless of where it might lead or what He might ask. Her whole life is a living proof of her compliance with God's will.

Jesus is the paragon of obedience, not only to His Father, but also to His earthly parents. St. Luke's statement is laconic, but revealing: "He [Jesus] went down with them then, and came to Nazareth, and was obedient to them" (*Luke 2:51*). Loving obedience to God and to each other certainly characterized every member of the Holy Family.

Secondly, that humble abode was a house of prayer. Scripture tells us that Mary pondered all these things in her heart. The Scriptures further remind us that the Holy Family went to the Temple in Jerusalem for all the Feasts "as was their custom." Surely, like every good Jew, they prayed the psalms daily and they lived in the presence of God constantly.

Surely loving care and concern for one another was the hallmark of the Holy Family. We can well imagine that loving concern which Joseph had for his charges. Jesus, in turn, reached out in love constantly to Mary and Joseph as He obeyed them. Can we imagine the sinless, unselfish Mary being anything other than a loving wife and mother?

The families in Israel, both Hebrew and Arabic, seem to be very closely knit families. The most important thing in their lives is their family. I wondered if this blessing was not part of the blessing the Holy Family left as their legacy.

I did pray earnestly for all the families I know, for all American families and all families around the world. Our homes must be the vestibules of heaven if we are to be a spiritually healthy nation. I left Nazareth reluctantly, but not before I placed every household living in Nazareth under the special patronage of Jesus, Mary and Joseph.

Together let us pray with the theme suggested by the following passages, but let us pray for all families constantly.

Luke 2:41-52 — *"His parents used to go every year to Jerusalem for the feast of the Passover. . . . "*

Matthew 2:19-23 — *"There he settled in a town called Nazareth."*

Proverbs 31:10-31 — *"When one finds a worthy wife, her value is far beyond pearls."*

Ephesians 5:22-33 — "Husbands, love your wives, as Christ loved the Church."

Ephesians 6:1-4 — "Children, obey your parents in the Lord. . . . "

Matthew 12:46-50 — "Whoever does the will of my heavenly Father is brother and sister and mother to me."

Colossians 3:18-21 — "You who are wives, be submissive to your husbands."

13. A Town Called Nazareth

"Jacob was the father of Joseph the husband of Mary. It was of her that Jesus who is called the Messiah was born" (Matthew 1:16).

St. Joseph was a carpenter. By this trade he supported the Holy Family at Nazareth. I am sure that Jesus also spent long hours at this trade. When the people were astounded at the wisdom and power of Jesus, they asked: "Is not this the carpenter, the son of Mary?" (*Mark 6:3*).

Today, carpenter shops abound in Nazareth even though wood is very scarce in this part of Israel. However, today the carpenter's trade has taken on some modern aspects. The scream of the electric saw and the whine of the jointer can be heard echoing through the narrow streets of Nazareth.

I paused to admire the work of a carpenter. His shop was a large room on the street level. It was part of a huge stone building which probably housed many families on the upper floors as well as a variety of shops on this first floor level.

Even though the language barrier allowed only limited communication, we were graciously received by this carpenter. His ready smile and his gracious attitude could easily take us back in memory to the foster father of Jesus. I am sure that Joseph was frequently interrupted in his work and I am equally certain that the reception he gave his intruders was most gracious.

A kind Franciscan brother took us to the home of Joseph. He pointed out the dwelling place of the Holy Family as well as the room which was used as the carpenter shop. Again this room was a part of a large stone complex which was probably shared by many families. The floor, walls and ceiling were all of stone.

As was our custom we spent some time in meditation and prayerful silence. I began to reflect on God's call to Joseph and his response to that call. Joseph was asked to step out in faith. He had been engaged to Mary, whom he loved dearly. Imagine his consternation and pain when Mary returned from the home of Zechariah and Elizabeth, and Joseph discovered that she was pregnant. What anxiety, torture, what doubt and disappointment must have gripped his heart! It could not possibly be true! What nightmares he must have experienced! What suffering in mind and heart!

God's ways are not our ways. When God calls us to a special vocation, there are so many ramifications which we cannot understand. In due time Joseph would learn of God's mysterious plan. Thus in our lives there can be so much fear and tension until we step out in faith and trust as God's unique plans begin to unravel. The quiet, unassuming role which Joseph played gives us much assurance.

During our prayer time this week, let us reflect on our own vocation from God and our response to it. May our prayer support us in the role to which God has called each one of us. May we derive inspiration and motivation, hope and encouragement, strength and perseverance from these giants in God's plan. May we come to realize that the role to which God has called us is equally important in His divine plan as was the role of these great giants in salvation history.

Let us prayerfully ponder our role in God's inscrutable plans.

Matthew 1:18-25 — "*Joseph, son of David, have no fear about taking Mary as your wife.*"

Matthew 2:13-15 — "*. . . the angel of the Lord suddenly appeared in a dream to Joseph with the command. . . .*"

Jeremiah 1:4-19 — "*Before I formed you in the womb I knew you. . . .*"

Genesis 12:1-9 — "*Go forth from the land of your kinsfolk. . . .*"

Matthew 2:19-23 — "*He got up, took the child and his mother, and returned to the land of Israel.*"

Isaiah 6:1-13 — "*Here I am . . . send me!*"

John 1:35-51 — "' *Follow me,' Jesus said to him.*"

14. Mount of Temptation

*"Not on bread alone is man to live
but on every utterance that comes
from the mouth of God" (Matthew 4:4).*

On our way to Jericho from Jerusalem we took the old Roman road which runs through the desert, and a real desert it is. Jesus used this road many times as He went to and from Jericho and Jerusalem. This way took us into the bleak and barren Judean hills. From this road we could see the Mount of Temptation. The Gospel tells us that after Jesus was baptized in the River Jordan, He was led by the Spirit into the desert. It is common tradition that Jesus prayed and fasted for 40 days on this mountain above Jericho. It was during this ordeal that He was tempted by the devil. Tradition established this flat-top mountain as the Mount of Temptation. It is also called Mount Quarantine, which means "forty."

There are several interesting sites on this mountain. About halfway up, clinging to the side of the mountain and overlooking a precipice, is a Greek Orthodox Monastery. It can be reached by a winding path. This monastery was built in front of the traditional grotto where Jesus prayed and fasted. A chapel venerates the place where Jesus spent His time in the desert. The stone on which Jesus was supposed to have sat is in a niche under the altar. This marks the site where the devil approached Jesus and asked Him to turn the stones into bread.

The summit of the mountain looks like a fortress because of the walls of a ruined medieval church which are still standing. The summit is supposed to be the spot where the third temptation took place, according to Matthew's account. In Luke it is the second temptation. "The devil then took him up a very high mountain and displayed before him all the kingdoms of the world in their magnificence."

As we reflect on this episode of the Gospel we may ask ourselves why Jesus had to endure these temptations. I am sure that there were many reasons and we can surmise some of them.

In the first place, Jesus was forming a new people. As the chosen people were tempted in the desert of Sinai, so the leader of the "new people" had to know temptation. The Israelites of old succumbed to temptation and deserted God to rally around pagan gods. God had to call them back to Him many times. However, Jesus came to conquer sin and death. In these temptations He proved to us that His power is infinite and that already sin is being conquered. Another reason, I am certain, is to give us an example. Just as Jesus was tempted, so, too, can we expect temptation in our life. Through trials and temptations we can grow and mature spiritually.

It is good to reflect on the nature of the temptations which the devil used to try to discover if Jesus was really God and also to test Him. In effect, the devil was asking Jesus not to establish His Kingdom according to God's plan, but to take the easy way. Surely there had to be an easier way. How often that same temptation comes to us. God's ways sometimes seem to be mysterious, difficult, different from the way we would expect Him to act or the way we ourselves would do things. There is much food for thought in this Gospel narrative.

When we reached the summit of the Mount of Temptation the view was absolutely breathtaking. The panorama was magnificent. The height gave us a whole new perspective. When we conquer temptation and say "yes" to God, our view changes radically. Temptation is usually self-centered. As we overcome temptation, our view becomes more cosmic. We are filled with the wonder and awe of God's divine design for us. With St. Paul we can say: "How deep are the riches and the wisdom and the knowledge of God! How inscrutable his judgments, how unsearchable his ways!" (*Romans 11:33*).

His Word will give us the wisdom and strength which we need to deal with temptation which is bound to occur in our lives.

Matthew 4:1-11 — *"You shall not put the Lord your God to the test."*

Deuteronomy 6:10-19 — *"The Lord, your God, shall you fear; him shall you serve. . . . "*

Hebrews 4:14-16 — *"So let us confidently approach the throne of grace to receive mercy and favor and to find help in time of need."*

Deuteronomy 8:1-20 — *". . . not by bread alone does man live, but by every word that comes forth from the mouth of the Lord."*

I Corinthians 10:1-13 — *"He will not let you be tested beyond your strength."*

II Peter 2:1-9 — *"The Lord, indeed, knows how to rescue devout men from trial. . . . "*

Hebrews 2:1-18 — *"Since he was himself tested through what he suffered, he is able to help those who are tempted."*

15. He Came to Nazareth

*". . . no prophet gains acceptance
in his native place" (Luke 4:24).*

Practically next door to the towering Basilica of
the Annunciation is the synagogue. It is a rather
small building made completely of stone. It will
accommodate less than 100 people standing. The
custodian was most hospitable. As we found seats
on the floor and also on a stone ledge, we reflected
quietly and privately on the scene which took
place here when Jesus returned to His hometown
of Nazareth.

After some time in meditation, I stood up on
what was once a kind of podium. From here I read
what St. Luke tells us of the tragedy of Nazareth.
Luke begins his account with the words: "He
[Jesus] came to Nazareth where he had been
reared, and entering the synagogue on the sabbath
as he was in the habit of doing, he stood up to do
the reading" (*Luke 4:14-30*). Here the tragic rejection of Nazareth begins to unfold. When Jesus announced that the passage of the prophet Isaiah ap-
plied to Him the audience was enraged. St. Luke
aptly records this pathetic event in these words:
"At these words the whole audience in the synagogue was filled with indignation. They rose up
and expelled him from the town, leading him to
the brow of the hill . . . intending to hurl him over
the edge."

This was one of the painful, heartrending rejections which Jesus was to receive throughout His
whole public life. How true the words of John:
"To his own he came, yet his own did not accept
him" (*John 1:11*).

Jesus left Nazareth, His own hometown, never
to return. A Franciscan brother reminded me that

probably Mary had to leave at the same time. Since her Son was rejected as a false prophet, she, too, would no longer be welcome and would have to find a home elsewhere.

Be with Mary as she gathers her few possessions together. Accompany her as she turns her steps away from the town in which she had lived so long. What memories were here: the visit by the Angel Gabriel, the warm, loving family with Jesus and Joseph, the many friends she had once as they met at the well which is now called Mary's Well. All this, however, was part and parcel of her total commitment to God. This, too, was included in her total "fiat."

As I finished reading Luke's account of the rejection of Jesus, I could see that there were few dry eyes in that little synagogue of Nazareth. I am not so sure my own eyes were not filled with tears.

As I sat I thought how many times I, too, have rejected Jesus. How many times less important priorities have taken over in my life. How frequently my time for prayer, to be alone with Jesus, was given over to less important tasks. How often my rest, my recreation, my self-will, my pleasure, my self-interest caused me to reject Jesus. How often I have relegated Jesus to a backseat in my life.

I paused to ask Jesus to forgive me and begged Mary to intercede for me that I might learn how to commit myself as generously as she did to her vocation.

I prayed, too, for all the people living in Nazareth at the present time that they, too, may accept Jesus. Let us ponder some of these rejections in our prayer for the next few days.

Luke 4:14-30 — "Today this Scripture passage is fulfilled in your hearing."

*John 6:60-69 — "From this time on, many of his
disciples broke away and would not remain in
his company any longer."*

*Mark 10:17-27 — "Then Jesus looked at him with
love . . . He [the man] went away sad. . . . "*

*Luke 22:54-62 — "The Lord turned around and
looked at Peter. . . . "*

*John 19:1-16 — "Away with him. . . . We have no
king but Caesar."*

*John 11:45-54 — "From that day onward there
was a plan afoot to kill him."*

*Mark 10:32-34 — "They will condemn him to
death. . . . "*

16. A Wedding in Cana

*"The cup of salvation I will take up,
and I will call upon the name
of the Lord . . . " (Psalm 116:13).*

A mention of the name "Cana of Galilee" always gives me a thrill, and I was excited as we set
out for this village. It is only five miles from Nazareth to Cana on the road to Tiberias. As we approached the village Kefar-Kana, or Cana, we
found a rather dense growth of cactus and many
pomegranate trees dotting the landscape. Today

the village is inhabited mostly by Arabs, both Christian and Moslem.

I have always held a warm spot in my heart for Cana of Galilee because of what took place there. There is a charm about the Gospel account of the wedding feast. There are many salutary lessons in this episode, even for us today.

At Nazareth, up to the age of 30, Jesus led a hidden life in perfect obedience to His parents. At Cana He began His public life by working His first miracle, that of changing water into wine. "Jesus performed this first of his signs at Cana in Galilee" (*John 2:11*). An English poet describes this first miracle in these words: "The modest water saw its God and blushed."

Here in Cana we experience the loving concern and solicitude of Mary for others. She did not want the bride and groom to be embarrassed by a scarcity of wine. We also learn of Mary's powerful intercession with her divine Son. At His mother's plea Jesus worked His first miracle even though His hour had not yet come. Thus Jesus taught us that He wants His mother to intercede for us, and also that He wants her to be the patroness of all who are in misery, want and suffering. Jesus also manifested His love and concern for others when He worked this first of His signs.

After spending some time in prayer, we celebrated the Holy Eucharist in the Franciscan Church in Cana. During the course of the Mass we witnessed another great miracle of Jesus. Here in this very spot water had been changed into wine; now for us Jesus changed wine into His own precious blood!

As we read John's Gospel account of the first of Jesus' signs and then spent time in reflection and prayer, a great joy welled up in my soul. I could almost hear Mary whispering to her Son: "They have no more wine." Jesus apparently refused her request, at least momentarily, but He did so to impress upon us the intercessory power of His mother and how He really wants us to approach Him through her. Mary understood this "apparent refusal" because with great poise and assurance she said to the waiters: "Do whatever he tells you."

Jesus responded to His mother's request, even though His hour had not yet come. It was an hour of grace and infinite mercy for all ages to come. This hour of Jesus was also the occasion of signing His own death warrant by working this first of many miracles, because already the envy and suspicion of His enemies were aroused.

We also visited the Chapel of St. Bartholomew. Bartholomew, or Nathanael of the Gospel, was a native of Cana. He was one of the first followers of Jesus, although he was not very enthusiastic about the newly found Messiah. His words live on in our memory: "Can anything good come from Nazareth?" (*John 1:46*). Since Nazareth was near Cana, Nathanael must have known something about the inhabitants of that village.

The Word of God is a powerful, transforming Word. As we pray with His Word, it can change the water of mediocrity in our lives into the pure wine of loving dedication. Jesus was speaking of His mother when He said in reply to the woman who praised Mary: "Rather, blest are they who hear the word of God and keep it" (*Luke 11:28*). May Mary, through her powerful intercession, obtain for us the grace not only to hear that Word, but also to keep it.

John 2:1-11 — "They have no more wine."

Isaiah 55:1-13 — "Come, without paying and without out cost, drink wine and milk!"

John 4:46-54 — *"This was the second sign that Jesus performed on returning from Judea to Galilee."*

Ephesians 5:18-21 — *"Avoid getting drunk on wine; . . . be filled with the Spirit. . . . "*

Luke 11:27-28 — *" 'Rather,' he replied, 'blest are they who hear the word of God and keep it.' "*

Sirach 32:1-6 — *"Like a gold mounting with an emerald seal is string music with delicious wine."*

John 1:35-51 — *"This man is a true Israelite."*

17. Peripatetic School at Capernaum

"He guides the humble to justice, he teaches the humble his way" (Psalm 25:9).

The day we set out for Capernaum there was both joy and sorrow in my heart. The history of Capernaum is one of great privilege, but also one of disappointment for its failure to respond to that privilege.

When Jesus was rejected as a false prophet in His hometown of Nazareth, He came to Capernaum to make His home here. The people of this town were unusually blessed and favored by His presence. I doubt that anyone ever saw Jesus in the flesh more frequently than did the inhabitants of Capernaum.

Here Jesus taught in season and out. They saw so many of His signs. He healed all who were brought to Him, whether suffering physically, spiritually or psychologically. They experienced His goodness and tenderness constantly. Yes, Capernaum was Jesus' second native place, the heart of His messianic work.

Jesus prayed with the people of Capernaum frequently when He joined them regularly in the synagogue. Even the synagogue was a special gift to them. It had been given them by a Roman centurion. Jesus prayed with and for these people as they gathered each Sabbath. They were the first to hear many of the truths He came to teach. They were also specially invited into His Kingdom.

It was here that Jesus expounded on the great gift which He was going to give them in the Eucharist (*John 6*). Here He called Matthew and thus proved His love for tax collectors and sinners. He reached out to sinners, especially at the banquet in Levi's house.

Many of the citizens of Capernaum heard many more of the teachings of Jesus, for they were just a stone's throw away from the Mount of the Beatitudes, where Jesus enunciated the heart of His messianic message. Just a few minutes' walk from Capernaum Jesus taught the crowd on the shore from the boat of St. Peter. They heard Jesus teach some of His most profound doctrines by the use of pastoral scenes around them: the vine and the branches, the fish of the sea, birds of the air and flowers of the field.

The very fact that Jesus chose to live at Capernaum proved that He really wanted to make these people His own. How truly the words of St. John apply to these inhabitants of Capernaum: "To his own he came, yet his own did not accept him" (*John 1:11*).

Jesus uttered a sad reproach and a terrible condemnation upon this unfaithful and ungrateful town: "And as for you, Capernaum, 'Are you to be exalted to the skies? You shall be hurled down to the realm of death!'" (*Luke 10:15*). This terrible fate which Jesus prophesied was not a threat, but a plea from His heart for the people to listen, to learn and to repent.

I sat for a long time in one of the stone seats of the synagogue, from which I could survey the excavations beyond the synagogue toward the lake. I began to wonder and my conscience pricked me as I pondered the fate of this town which Jesus loved. What God has done for me! The years I have been given to study His teachings, the hours I have had the luxury of spending with Him in prayer, the countless times I have been privileged to offer Eucharist and to receive Him eucharistically, the myriad times I have experienced His mystical presence — all this touched me deeply.

However, I immediately felt the reassurance which Jesus gives us. He does not look at the results of our response to His invitation; all He asks is our willingness to listen and to respond. That thought brought me great comfort and encouragement.

As we experience the presence of Jesus in His Word, let us come with eager hearts not only to listen to Him, but to translate His message into practice in our own lives. Let us remember, too, that all that Jesus asks of us is our willingness to live in harmony with His teaching.

Mark 1:14-22 — "Reform your lives and believe in the Gospel!"

Mark 4:1-20 — "What the sower is sowing is the word."

John 6:25-51 — "I myself am the living bread come down from heaven."

Matthew 18:1-14 — " . . . unless you change and become like little children, you will not enter the kingdom of God."

Mark 9:33-50 — "If anyone wishes to rank first, he must remain the last one of all and the servant of all."

Matthew 18:15-20 — "Where two or three are gathered in my name, there am I in their midst."

Luke 5:33-39 — "New wine should be poured into fresh skins."

18. Signs at Capernaum

*" . . . no man can perform signs and wonders
such as you perform
unless God is with him" (John 3:2).*

The town of Capernaum is situated along the shore of the Sea of Galilee in one of the most picturesque parts of Israel. At Capernaum we were hosted by a Franciscan priest-archeologist who has been working on the excavations and who was knowledgeable about the findings during the past few years. Archeologists have uncovered a syna-

Sea of Galilee.

gogue which dates back to the first century. However, it was probably built later than the one in which Our Lord taught and prayed. At the present time archeologists are exploring the possibility that the synagogue which Jesus frequented might have been under the foundation of this existing one. The priest-archeologist explained many exciting things to us. We saw the stone olive and wine presses which the people used. Many of the poor homes were being excavated and we could see what the town looked like. Of special interest was the home of St. Peter. This good priest took hours away from his work to guide us through the excavated ruins of this town, which was once the second hometown of Jesus.

Capernaum was the site and witness of many of the miracles of Jesus. Here in the synagogue He cured the man possessed by an unclean spirit. Jesus healed the paralytic who was let down through the roof in front of Him. Jesus was deeply touched by the faith of the men who had brought the paralytic to Him. His healing reached beyond His own people. When the Roman centurion's servant was seriously ill he asked the Jewish leaders to beg Jesus to heal his servant. Jesus went without hesitation. When the centurion met Jesus he said humbly: "Sir . . . do not trouble yourself, for I am not worthy to have you enter my house" (*Luke 7:6*). These words have been immortalized in the Mass just before Holy Communion. These are but a few of the miracles which Jesus worked here in Capernaum, in order to bring health and happiness to bodies and minds.

As I sat on a large stone in the midst of the ruins of this once-flourishing and favored town, all these events came to mind. It was easy to visualize some of these happenings. The remains of the narrow streets and the walls of former habitable buildings could tell many stories of the loving solicitude and concern of Jesus for those people.

Between the walls of Capernaum and the seashore not too many yards away, a beautiful grove of eucalyptus trees forms a natural outdoor sanctuary. In the center of this grove is a little altar. Here we gathered to celebrate the Eucharist and to make Jesus eucharistically present with us in this, His favorite spot.

During the celebration, all nature obliged and joined in our hymn of praise to the Father. The water kept lapping the shoreline, purifying and cleansing it. A gentle breeze brought cool relief and caused the leaves to rustle ever so gently, adding their voice to our liturgy. The many birds in this part of the country formed a perfect choir with their own particular song of praise. All of this spoke to us, for we seemed to be in a reverent, festive mood as we rejoiced to have the eucharistic Jesus with us and within us.

We relived all the divine happenings of Capernaum in our prayer. We were with Jesus in Capernaum, hearing His words, seeing Him move among the people, rejoicing at His healing power.

The writer of the Letter to the Hebrews tells us that Jesus is the same yesterday, today and forever. We know that the same Jesus who loved Capernaum and all its inhabitants is dwelling among us with an even greater and deeper presence. His Word gives us that assurance.

Mark 2:1-12 — "When Jesus saw their faith, he said to the paralyzed man, 'My son, your sins are forgiven.'"

Luke 7:1-10 — "... I am not worthy to have you enter my house."

69

Mark 1:23-28 — "A completely new teaching in a spirit of authority!"

Mark 3:1-16 — "Is it permitted to do a good deed on the sabbath — or an evil one?"

Matthew 9:18-26 — ". . . he entered and took her by the hand, and the little girl got up."

John 6:1-15 — "Get the people to recline."

Matthew 14:22-33 — "How little faith you have . . . Why did you falter?"

19. Mount of Beatitudes

*". . . blest are they who hear the word of God
and keep it" (Luke 11:28).*

One of the most precious memories I have of all of Israel is my visit to the Mount of Beatitudes. What took place here is told by St. Matthew as he introduces the Sermon on the Mount. "When he [Jesus] saw the crowds he went up on the mountainside. After he had sat down his disciples gathered around him, and he began to teach them" (*Matthew 5:1*).

What a gorgeous spot Jesus chose for this important teaching — the Magna Carta of Christianity. Situated on a slope overlooking the Sea of Galilee is the Beautiful Church of the Beatitudes, which marks the traditional site of this teaching. The shrine is octagonal in shape and commemorates the Eight Beatitudes, one of which is inscribed on each of the windows. The dome over the altar glitters with a gold mosaic. An arched ambulatory with large windows gives one a commanding view of the lake from all sides. The surrounding slopes are covered with groves of trees, especially orange, almond and banana trees. The fertile countryside is also patterned with vineyards and vegetable gardens. It is a picturesque site and one which will linger long in my memory.

We were fortunate to be able to spend nearly two weeks here as guests of the Italian Franciscan nuns who own and operate the chapel and hospice. What an ideal place for prayer! There is a mystic silence and a heavenly peace about this sanctuary, which together with the "Sea of Jesus" is vaulted with a crystal-blue sky. Jesus sanctified these fields by His presence, by His teachings and by His signs and wonders. How good it was to roam the gentle slopes carpeted and aglow with the enchanting flowers of spring.

The garden, too, with its lush blossoms and flowers provided a prayerful environment. Early in the morning our prayer was accompanied by the singing of birds, especially mourning doves. They sang their praises to God as they greeted the rising sun across the lake. The sights and sounds were most conducive to prayer.

Many of the important places along the Sea of Galilee where Jesus taught and worked His miracles were within easy walking distance from the Casa Nova. There were many paths threading their way through the fragrant orchards and the blossoming vineyards.

Each morning some of our retreatants could be seen walking alone and contemplatively down the slope toward the lake. It was a delightful picture to see them silhouetted along the shore as the sun began to rise over the lake. It was not uncommon to see others sitting in various parts of the gardens, in vineyards and orchards, as they raised their hearts to God in prayer.

It would be difficult to single out the principal highlight of our sojourn on the Mount of Beatitudes. The first one which comes to mind was the morning when a friend and I offered the Holy Sacrifice of the Mass in one of the vineyards. The budding vines spoke so beautifully of the fruit of the vine which Jesus had chosen for the Eucharist. The rays of the rising sun radiating across the lake reflected God's loving presence. The melodious song of the birds singing *viva voce* formed a perfect choir for our celebration.

From our improvised altar of sacrifice I could see an Arab father accompanied by his family going out to work in the fields. As I closed my eyes I could readily visualize Jesus walking along with His disciples, the crowds following. When my attention was attracted to a shepherd leading his flock to green pastures, I could hear the words of Jesus calling Himself the Good Shepherd who lovingly cares for His sheep. Our garden spot in the vineyard was truly a sanctuary hallowed by the beauty of His creation and sanctified by His eucharistic presence. It was a morning not soon to be forgotten.

What a gorgeous place for Jesus to choose to announce the real heart of the Christian message summarized in the Beatitudes! How diametrically different is this message from the attitude of the world! How much the Christian must stand apart as he lives the spirit of these Beatitudes! Just as the Beatitudes are the source of joy and happiness to the Christian, so the beauty of this portion of the Holy Land brings peace and joy to the heart of the prayerful pilgrim.

Listen intently to what Jesus is saying to you in this lengthy teaching on the Mount of Beatitudes.

Matthew 5:3-12 — *"How blest are the poor in spirit: the reign of God is theirs."*

Matthew 5:13-16 — *"You are the light of the world."*

Matthew 5:43-48 — *"My command to you is: love your enemies, pray for your persecutors."*

Matthew 6:5-51 — *"If you forgive the faults of others, your heavenly Father will forgive you yours."*

Matthew 6:25-34 — *"Seek first his kingship over you, his way of holiness, and all these things will be given you besides."*

Matthew 7:7-11 — *". . . how much more will your heavenly Father give good things to anyone who asks him!"*

Matthew 7:12-23 — *"Treat others the way you would have them treat you. . . . "*

20. Apples of Sodom

*"Every tree that is not fruitful
will be cut down and
thrown into the fire" (Luke 3:9).*

One day as we were walking from Bethany back to Jerusalem we were reminded that Jesus had walked this route many times, especially toward the end of His earthly life. He would go into the city to teach and perform His signs; then He "went out of the city to Bethany, where he spent the night" (*Matthew 21:17*).

On one such morning, Jesus taught a very valuable lesson. "At dawn, as Jesus was returning to the city, he felt hungry. Seeing a fig tree by the roadside he went over to it, but found nothing there except leaves. He said to it, 'Never again shall you produce fruit!' and it withered up instantly" (*Matthew 21:18-19*).

There is a perpetual reminder of this lesson in Israel even today. During our visit we discovered a plant which has been appropriately named the Apple of Sodom. This is a seed-bearing plant with bright, luscious, red blooms. The plant blooms in late spring or early summer and is beautiful to behold. In spite of its gorgeous color, it bears no useful fruit other than a kind of shell. As you break open the shell, you find a fibrous interior containing a few seeds. The shell is dry. There is nothing edible in this fruit.

Its name, the Apple of Sodom, is certainly biblical and speaks for itself. Sodom was a city which bore no fruit. It was destroyed by God, along with its sister city, Gomorrah. " . . . the Lord rained down sulphurous fire upon Sodom and Gomorrah. He overthrew those cities and the whole Plain, together with the inhabitants of the cities and the produce of the soil . . . he [Abraham] saw dense smoke over the land rising like fumes from a furnace" (*Genesis 19:24ff*). Jesus cursing the fig tree teaches us the same lesson.

Many times Jesus reminded us that we must be willing to cooperate with Him in bringing forth good fruit. In the Sermon on the Mount Jesus outlined a whole series of parables warning us that only through good works will we find the way of life that will eventually lead us to the happiness which the Father has in store for us.

Jesus certainly taught us the necessity of our producing good fruit. Our lives must witness to our Christian living. However, we must be careful not to misunderstand the lesson Jesus was trying to teach us.

In the first place we cannot produce good fruit of ourselves. There is frequently a notion that we must work out our own salvation, that our salvation depends on our own efforts. If we simply try harder to rid ourselves of certain faults and imperfections and make greater efforts to practice certain virtues, then we will be producing good fruit. Jesus reminded us that without Him we can do nothing, and He meant just that.

Secondly, we may have the notion that we must get involved in feverish activity in order to accumulate enough "brownie points" to earn our heavenly reward. This kind of "bookkeeping spirituality" is equally wrong.

Salvation is a gift from God. We cannot merit it, we cannot earn it. We do not deserve it. Our salvation is pure gift. St. Paul says: "It is God's gift; neither is it a reward for anything you accomplished" (*Ephesians 2:8f*).

All that God asks of us is our cooperation. Our Abba is a sensitive Father. He will not force a gift into a clenched hand. We must open ourselves to receive His gift. We must put forth that ascetical effort to keep ourselves pliable like clay in the potter's hands so that God can accomplish in us what He wills. We must "let God."

In the encouraging parable of the vine and the branches, Jesus tells us that it is the branch which blossoms out and bears fruit; but that would obviously be impossible if the branch did not stay attached to the life-giving vine. What a lesson for us!

As we come before our loving Father with an openness, with a genuine *kenosis* or real poverty of spirit and let Him work the miracles of His grace in us, then we will bear good fruit. Let the Apples of Sodom speak to us.

Matthew 7:15-23 — "*You can tell a tree by its fruit.*"

John 15:1-8 — "*My Father has been glorified in your bearing much fruit. . . .*"

Ephesians 2:1-10 — "*This is not your own doing, it is God's gift. . . .*"

I Corinthians 1:26-31 — "*God it is who has given you life in Christ Jesus.*"

Matthew 21:18-22 — "*Never again shall you produce fruit!*"

Luke 13:6-9 — "*Sir, leave it another year, while I hoe around it. . . .*"

Matthew 12:33-37 — "*Declare a tree good and its fruit good or declare a tree rotten and its fruit rotten. . . .*"

Colossians 1:9-14 — "You will multiply good works of every sort. . . . "

21. The House of St. Peter

"Simon Peter, servant and apostle
of Jesus Christ, to those who have been given
a faith like ours in the justifying power
of our God and Savior Jesus Christ;
may grace be yours and peace in abundance
through your knowledge of God
and of Jesus, our Lord" (II Peter 1:1-2).

One of the most interesting discoveries for me at Capernaum was to learn that the house in which St. Peter lived has been found. It was only within the last few years that this site was excavated and authenticated. It is well substantiated that the early Judaeo-Christian community venerated this house as the home of Peter and that they gathered there regularly for worship. In a complex of very poor dwellings, one hall is known to be the House of St. Peter. By the first century it had already become a sort of shrine.

There is sufficient evidence to prove that this is actually the place where Peter lived. The symbols incised within the house, the graffiti on the walls and the mosaics on the floor, as well as other scientific data, prove conclusively that this building was venerated as the home of St. Peter. The excavations also reveal that an ancient church was built over this spot, possibly in the fifth century. It was built in two concentric octagons with a portico on five sides. This church was built around and over the House of St. Peter.

When Jesus was expelled from His hometown of Nazareth after His appearance in the synagogue (*Luke 4*), He came to live at Capernaum and established His headquarters here. A strong tradition holds that Jesus lived right here in the home of St. Peter. How His physical presence sanctified that house! What a privilege to welcome Jesus into that home! What a Guest, the transcendent God of heaven and earth, living here in His humanity!

As I sat on the stone wall overlooking the House of St. Peter, I pondered what a momentous occasion it must have been for the members of Peter's family and for the citizens of this town to have had Jesus living with them and among them. In my mind's eye I could see Jesus walking down the narrow stone street. In fact, the street is so narrow that a man standing in the center of the street and extending his arms could probably have touched the walls on either side. I thought of the cure of the woman with the issue of blood. When she touched the cloak of Jesus He turned and asked who had touched Him. The disciples were surprised at the question, but Jesus asked it simply to let the bystanders know that He was healing this poor woman.

As I pondered how privileged these people were to have had Jesus live with them, to teach, heal and love them, a tinge of envy arose in me. I wished I could see Jesus here and now with His apostles, coming down this narrow passageway which was called a street. This thought and these feelings of envy soon passed when I realized once again what a great privilege is mine.

The reason is this: by Baptism we are all totally immersed into the Trinitarian life. The Risen Jesus

78

is more alive and more present to us than He had been in His physical form before His Resurrection and appearances to His apostles and friends. Jesus is living and dwelling within us, nurturing, encouraging and loving us.

The House of St. Peter is a precious relic and one very dear to the heart of every Christian. My body, on the other hand, is the very temple of the Holy Spirit. I heard Paul say once again: "Are you not aware that you are the temple of God, and that the Spirit of God dwells in you . . . " (*I Corinthians 3:16*). On another occasion Paul reminds us that we are the sons of God because of the indwelling of the Holy Spirit within us. This is the great gift which we received at the moment of our Baptism when we were immersed into the divine life: "All of you who have been baptized into Christ have clothed yourselves with him" (*Galatians 3:27*). This is what gives us our dignity as Christians. This makes us important to God: we are His adopted sons and daughters.

I was very much encouraged by these reminders coming from the Apostle of the Gentiles as I sat there surveying the House of St. Peter. Our prayerful reflection will keep us ever aware of this sublime truth.

Luke 4:31-41 — "Leaving the synagogue, he entered the house of Simon."

Mark 1:14-22 — "Come after me; I will make you fishers of men."

Matthew 17:24-27 — "Open its mouth and you will discover there a coin worth twice the temple tax."

Mark 10:17-31 — "We have put aside everything to follow you!"

Matthew 4:12-22 — "He left Nazareth and went down to live in Capernaum. . . . "

I Corinthians 3:10-23 — ". . . you are Christ's, and Christ is God's."

Romans 8:14-17 — "All who are led by the Spirit of God are sons of God."

22. Multiplication of the Loaves — Loving Concern

*"He rained manna upon them for food
and gave them heavenly bread"
(Psalm 78:24).*

Our stay at the Sea of Galilee was most rewarding. The countryside surrounding the lake was in the full bloom of spring. Here Jesus spent much of His public life. Around this great lake Jesus taught patiently for endless hours. He healed all those afflicted who were brought to Him. Here, also, He performed many of His signs and wonders.

On a beautiful spring morning we set out for Et Tabgha. Our destination was the place where Jesus first nourished thousands of hungry hearts with His Word and then provided for their physical well-

Tabgha — site of the **Miracle of Loaves and Fishes.**

being by multiplying the loaves and fishes to satisfy their hunger.

Et Tabgha is a corruption of the Greek word "heptapegon," meaning "seven springs." Today there is a beautiful landscaped villa here and the irrigation water from the springs is plentiful. At the time of Jesus it was a deserted area without homes or civilization.

Today a modest church is built over the site where Jesus multiplied the loaves and fishes to feed 5,000 men. One of the German Benedictine monks, who have a little monastery next to the church, hosted us and guided us through the church.

Under the altar we found a large stone on which Jesus was supposed to have placed the bread and the fish as He prayed and gave thanks to His Father before distributing the bread to the people. It was a joy and a privilege to be able to see, to touch and to kiss this stone which was so sanctified by the touch of Jesus.

The multiplication of the loaves was only one of many miracles which Jesus performed in this general location. All of His miracles teach us some valuable lessons. The multiplication of the loaves is no exception.

In the first place, Jesus manifested His loving concern for these people by supplying their physical needs after He had fed them with His Word. Many of these people were pilgrims on their way to Jerusalem for the Passover. This site was along the road which the pilgrims were accustomed to taking on their way to the Temple and the Holy City. As some were far from home, it is understandable that they had no food with them. It is also understandable why they tarried so long. They had heard much about the great Prophet who had come and they were most anxious to see and hear Him. His magnetic personality and the hope which His teaching held out to them made them forget time and human needs.

Jesus used this occasion not only to manifest His divine power but, more importantly, to demonstrate His loving concern for them. He showed His providential love by satisfying their hunger. Yes, He performed this sign to prepare His disciples and all those who heard Him for the greatest of all His gifts: the gift of Himself in the Holy Eucharist. He had already proved His power over water by changing water into wine at the wedding feast in Cana. He now showed His power over bread by multiplying the loaves to feed this incredibly large crowd. This sign was a preparation for the great gift of His love: the Eucharist.

The loving concern of Jesus extends far beyond these people on the shore of the Sea of Galilee, and also far beyond those who were present with Him at the Last Supper when He gave them His body to eat and His blood to drink. His loving concern is universal and eternal. It is also exclusive, for it reaches down through the centuries to you and to me, personally.

Jesus amply supplies our temporal needs as we pray, "Give us this day our daily bread." Daily, hourly, even moment by moment He nurtures us with His powerful Word. Each day, He comes to us eucharistically to nourish our souls.

These were some of the thoughts which came to mind as we visited this hallowed spot. May you capture some of the loving concern of Jesus as you pray these suggested texts:

John 6:1-15 — "Not even with two hundred days' wages could we buy loaves enough to give each of them a mouthful!"

Exodus 16:4-15 — *"This is the bread which the Lord has given you to eat."*

Luke 8:40-56 — *". . . he told them to give her something to eat."*

Matthew 6:25-34 — *"Your heavenly Father knows all that you need."*

Luke 22:7-20 — *"This is my body to be given for you. Do this as a remembrance of me."*

John 6:25-58 — *"I myself am the bread of life. No one who comes to me shall ever be hungry. . . ."*

Matthew 15:32-38 — *"My heart is moved with pity for the crowd."*

23. Multiplication of the Loaves — Trust

*"We were left to feel like men
condemned to death
so that we might trust,
not in ourselves, but in God
who raises the dead" (II Corinthians 1:9).*

Many tourists come to the Church of the Multiplication of the Loaves at Et Tabgha on the shore of the Sea of Galilee. As the tourist enters the church, he soon becomes a prayerful pilgrim. Such is the influence of sacred places like this one. The ancient mosaics found here help to put a person in a reflective, prayerful mood.

The floor of the church is covered with many beautiful mosaics. The mosaics depict the flora and fauna of bygone days. The antiquity and the beauty of these mosaics help us to recall God's gentle dealing with His people.

A mosaic which really touched me was the magnificent mosaic between the altar and the apse of the church. This work of art is quite simple, but its message is rich and powerful. In the center of this mosaic is a large basket filled with loaves of bread, flanked on either side by a fish. What a testimonial to the loving concern of Jesus!

Jesus used this occasion to teach the apostles a valuable lesson. As the hours glided by the people showed no inclination to leave, so moved were they by His teaching. The apostles were getting anxious. Finally they came to Jesus and asked Him to dismiss the crowd so that they could find something to eat. In turn Jesus asked them why they did not supply the food for this crowd to eat. You can imagine how startled they must have been at His question! They must have smiled at the impossibility of their feeding this huge crowd, and they asked: "Are we to go and spend two hundred days' wages for bread to feed them?" (*Mark 6:37*). Jesus wanted them to admit their own helplessness, their own inability to supply such an astronomical amount of food.

It was only after they had admitted their own inadequacy, their own poverty of spirit, that Jesus came to their rescue.

What a lesson for us! As long as we strive to accomplish all things ourselves, we are bound to fail sooner or later. Once we recognize our own poverty of spirit and come to Jesus with trust and faith, then will He supply all our needs. Yes, He wants us to put forth our best efforts, but He also wants us to recognize that we could not even desire to put forth our best efforts were it not for His giving us that desire. That's what Paul meant when he said: "It is God who, in his good will toward you, begets in you any measure of desire or achievement" (*Philippians 2:13*).

Jesus also wanted to test the faith of both the apostles and the people when He asked the people to sit down. This was an acid test. They were tired, restless and weary from travelling. They were hungry. They knew that if they sat down, they were helpless.

I am sure that when the order came for the people to sit down in groups, all present did not respond instantly. I am certain that some did sit down immediately while others hesitated and had some misgivings about this strange request. No doubt some were even resentful and may have complained vehemently. Finally the whole crowd sat down. In itself this is a miracle of faith. Five thousand men placed their trust in Jesus. Five thousand men said, "Yes, I believe that He can and will do something for us."

What a lesson of trust! What a lesson of faith! These hungry, tired people trusted Jesus. Once they manifested their faith in Him, Jesus responded most generously to their need.

Today Jesus is equally concerned about our every need, be it infinitesimal or monumental. He wants our faith and trust. He wants us to recognize our poverty of spirit. Jesus, like the rest of us, needs to be needed. When we come with our needs He responds most graciously and most generously.

Our problem is that we have become so self-sufficient and forget so easily about our complete dependence upon God for every heartbeat, for every thought which enters our mind. One of my friends frequently reminds me of this truth when he tells me: "Fear not! You *are* inadequate."

With these people at Tabgha, let us sit down. Let us sit at the feet of Jesus and listen to His Word:

Mark 6:34-44 — *"The people took their places in hundreds and fifties, neatly arranged like flower beds."*

John 15:1-8 — *"... apart from me you can do nothing."*

John 14:1-6 — *"Have faith in God and faith in me."*

Mark 8:14-21 — *"They had forgotten to bring any bread along. ..."*

Matthew 11:2-6 — *"Go back and report to John what you hear and see. ..."*

Mark 9:14-29 — *"Everything is possible to a man who trusts."*

Luke 12:22-32 — *"How much more important you are than the birds!"*

24. Confession of Peter — Promise of Primacy

"For God's folly is wiser than men,
and his weakness more powerful than men"
(I Corinthians 1:25).

Caesarea Philippi strikes a resonant chord in the hearts of many of us. It was here that Jesus asked a very pointed question of the apostles: "And you, who do you say that I am?" Peter, in his usual eager and impetuous manner, responded emphatically in the name of all the apostles: "You are the Messiah, the Son of the living God."

Banias, or Caesarea Philippi, is in the northern-most part of Israel. It is close to Mount Hermon and is a sort of panhandle separating Syria and Lebanon. We journeyed there to visit the site where St. Peter had made his public profession of faith and to see the sources of the River Jordan.

Caesarea Philippi is a strange site chosen by Jesus to ask this question of the apostles. On the other hand, it is a most appropriate one. In this location was a large grotto built to worship the pagan god Pan. Here the people were called to pagan worship by the pipes of Pan. Captivating carousal stirred up the people and eventually led them into panic and anarchy. On this same spot Jesus promised Peter that he would be the future leader of His Church. Under Peter's leadership the Church was to strive to accomplish the direct opposite of pagan worship. By proclaiming the Good News, peace and tranquility, law and order would be enjoyed by men.

However, Peter had to be further conditioned for that leadership. He was still a man beset with all the weaknesses to which our sinful humanity is subject. When Jesus prophesied that He would have to suffer and die, Peter protested so violently that Jesus said he still had the mind of Satan. When Jesus advised Peter to pray that he would not be led into the temptation of denying His Master, Peter stated emphatically and unequivocally that even though all the rest would deny Him, he, Peter, would not. That was the beginning of his fall. In the Garden of Gethsemane, immediately after receiving the Holy Eucharist for the first time, Peter failed to support His Master in prayer and promptly fell asleep. A few hours later he denied that he even knew Jesus. These were the disappointing and disastrous failings of a weak human being. What a drastic change in Peter after the Resurrection and the coming of the Holy Spirit upon him!

At Caesarea Philippi we assembled in a large cave for the celebration of the Eucharist. It was an unusual setting for our Mass, but one which made the presence of Jesus very real for me. We sought shelter from a misty rain which was falling intermittently and protection against a chilly breeze. I thought how Jesus and His apostles must have done the same as they journeyed up and down the countryside.

In this cave a table-sized rock with a flat top served ideally as an altar for our Liturgy. As the words of Scripture resounded throughout the cave, I was reminded that most certainly the voice of Jesus had re-echoed in this same cave which had been sanctified by His physical presence. His Eucharistic presence at Mass brought to mind a vision of Jesus surrounded by His apostles and His direct question to them: "Who do people say that the Son of Man is?"

My reflection that morning seemed to dwell on the person of Peter. I could identify so easily with him! All too often I have followed the same pattern. How often I have failed Jesus! I have depended upon my own talent and ability, my own strength and resoluteness, only to fail miserably.

I find great hope and consolation in Peter's impetuosity and weakness. His human failings prepared him for the office for which Jesus was training him. These weaknesses made Peter docile, humble and more sympathetic about the failures of others.

Like Peter I get in the Lord's way. I pray that, like Peter, I may profit from my weakness so that God may use me in His divine plan.

Let us pray, too, that all of us may listen to God's Word in prayer so that we may respond to the question which Jesus is putting to us: "And you, who do you say that I am?"

Matthew 16:13-20 — ". . . you are 'Rock,' and on this rock I will build my church. . . . "

Luke 5:1-11 — "Do not be afraid. From now on you will be catching men."

John 1:35-42 — "You are Simon, son of John; your name shall be Cephas (which is rendered Peter)."

Matthew 19:23-30 — "Then it was Peter's turn to say to him: 'Here we have put everything aside to follow you.' "

Matthew 16:21-28 — "May you be spared, Master! God forbid that any such thing ever happen to you!"

Luke 22:54-62 — "The Lord turned around and looked at Peter. . . . "

John 13:1-17 — " 'Lord,' Simon Peter said to him, 'then not only my feet, but my hands and head as well.' "

25. Jacob's Well

" . . . the water I give shall become a fountain within him, leaping up to provide eternal life" (John 4:14).

"He [Jesus] had to pass through Samaria, and his journey brought him to a Samaritan town named Schechem" (*John 4:4*). Jesus entered the country of the Samaritans, like Abraham many centuries before, by going through the valley between Mount Gerizim and Mount Ebal. Our journey took us over the same route. When we arrived at the town of Schechem we proceeded to the synagogue, where the Samaritans greeted us warmly. They proudly displayed for us what they claim is the oldest manuscript of the Pentateuch (the first five books of the Bible). They were eager to explain their history and their customs and beliefs. There are only about 250 Samaritans left in the world and they have so intermarried that they are no longer a healthy tribe of people. After a short visit with them we continued our journey to Jacob's Well.

This well is famous in biblical lore. After Abraham, Jacob bought a piece of property here and dug a well for his flocks. This well and territory Jacob bequeathed to Joseph. Later Joseph's body was brought from Egypt to be buried here. This spot was always venerated by the Jews until it was taken over by the Christians. Through the centuries the well has always amply supplied the people of this area. Today the well and the partially finished church have been acquired by the Greek Orthodox.

We entered the areas surrounded by the partially finished walls of the church. From what might be called the nave of the church we descended a stairway down to the well itself. It has retained much of its original flavor. You can draw water with a rope and bucket. I discovered that the well is about 160 feet deep; hence the Samaritan woman was right when she said to Jesus: "Sir, you do not have a bucket and this well is deep." We drew some water and drank from the well. We visited briefly and spent some time in the surrounding gardens.

Our brief visit and the time we spent in meditation as we travelled along brought back many reflections on the enlightening images Jesus used of "living water." Jesus frequently used the term "living water" to explain the divine life that He was going to share with us.

Many lessons can be drawn from the images Jesus presented. Water is absolutely essential to all forms of life — plant, animal and human. Jesus used this metaphor to explain that just as we cannot live without natural water, so we cannot live spiritually without "living water," His divine life. Just as physical life is sustained by water, so must our spiritual life be well watered by His presence and power within us. This is what Jesus meant when He told the Samaritan woman that He would have given her living water if she had asked for it.

Water is also a cleansing and purifying substance. Continuing the analogy, we are purified by the "living water" of the divine life which Jesus sheds so abundantly upon us; this forgiving, healing and redeeming "living water" is the source of our peace, joy, strength, life and love.

As we come into the dazzling, luminous presence of Jesus, we can see ourselves more clearly in our relationship to Him. When the Samaritan woman came into the presence of Jesus she recognized her sinfulness more acutely. Jesus was ever so gentle with her. He opened her heart by first asking a favor from her: "Give me a drink." Jesus leads us gently to recognize our weaknesses, our faults and failings, so that we may be cleansed by His "living water."

During our time of prayer may we come to Jacob's Well to be nourished, cleansed and strengthened by the "living water" which is Jesus Himself.

John 4:4-42 — *"This was the site of Jacob's well. Jesus, tired from his journey, sat down at the well."*

Genesis 29:1-14 — *"[Jacob] . . . saw a well in the open country, with three droves of sheep huddled near it, for droves were watered from that well."*

Matthew 10:1-42 — *" . . . whoever gives a cup of cold water to one of these lowly ones because he is a disciple will not want for his reward."*

Psalm 36:1-13 — *"For with you is the fountain of life, and in your light we see light."*

John 7:37-52 — *"If anyone thirsts, let him come to me. . . . "*

Isaiah 58:1-14 — *" . . . you shall be like a watered garden, like a spring whose water never fails."*

Matthew 25:31-46 — ". . . when did we see you hungry and feed you or see you thirsty and give you drink?"

26. Revelation at Jacob's Well

*"Are you the Messiah,
the Son of the Blessed One? . . .
I am . . . " (Mark 14:61).*

One day as we journeyed from Jerusalem to Galilee we, like Jesus, came "to a Samaritan town named Shechem. . . . This was the site of Jacob's well. Jesus, tired from his journey, sat down at the well" (*John 4:4ff*). Even though our modern comfortable mode of travelling was far less fatiguing than the journey Jesus made on foot, nevertheless we, too, were tired from our journey. Like Jesus, we also were refreshed by the cool water drawn from Jacob's Well in a bucket let down by a rope.

A beautiful garden surrounds the well, which is located in a partially finished church. I found a quite prayerful spot amid the flowering trees in the garden. I sat down to relax and pray. As I read John's account of the encounter of Jesus with the Samaritan woman I discovered anew how sensitively Jesus revealed Himself to this poor woman. He reached out in love to her by asking her for a favor: "Give me a drink." He gradually opened her heart and made her receptive to the divine revelation which He was about to make to her.

The Samaritan woman began to recognize something unusual about this Jewish stranger and admitted, "I can see you are a prophet." Finally, when she asked about the Messiah, Jesus identified Himself: "I who speak to you am he."

My heart leaped with joy as I heard Jesus speak these words. I was thrilled that Jesus revealed Himself to this woman. Jesus reached out in love to her and she became an apostle of love to the people of her village. Jesus always makes Himself known to the *anawim*, the little people, the people unimportant in the eyes of the world, the people who come to Him with a real poverty of spirit.

Then numerous other thoughts crowded into my mind. I began reflecting on the many times Jesus made Himself known by saying "I am. . . . " It was time to go now, but as I travelled in the bus I began rereading and reflecting on the many occasions when Jesus revealed something about Himself by saying "I am. . . . "

We can get to know a person better by what he says about himself as he speaks to us. By his conversation he often tells us about his hopes and ambitions, about his joys and sorrows. He also reveals much about his personality and his character. This is precisely what Jesus did. On many occasions by His words Jesus revealed something about Himself. As we come to listen to His Word, we can really get to know Him as a person.

In the "I am" passages Jesus tells us of His loving concern for each one of us. He gives us directives and norms which will lead us to a happy, peaceful life as we follow in His footsteps. In picturesque and figurative language, He gives us a keener insight into the mystery of His divinity. Principally, He tells us that He is a gracious, compassionate God who loves us with an infinite love.

When we get to know Jesus as a person, then we can more easily establish an intimate personal relationship with Him. Praying and listening to His Word will keep us ever aware of His abiding presence with us and within us. Like the disciples on the road to Emmaus, we do not always recognize Him until we invite Him to stay with us, until we invite Him to speak to us through His Word.

Each day as you listen prayerfully to what He is saying about Himself in these suggested scriptural readings, you will discover many dimensions in the person of Jesus which you really never knew before. It will be an exhilarating discovery.

John 10:1-16 — *"I am the good shepherd."*

John 8:12-20 — *"I am the light of the world."*

John 14:6-7 — *"I am the way, and the truth, and the life. . . . "*

John 15:1-17 — *"I am the true vine. . . . "*

John 6:35-40 — *"I myself am the bread of life."*

John 11:1-44 — *"I am the resurrection and the life. . . . "*

John 4:4-42 — *"I who speak to you am he."*

27. Naim

"Young man, I bid you get up" (Luke 7:14).

Naim is a village in Galilee at the foot of Little Hermon about eight miles from Nazareth and approximately 30 miles from Capernaum. The name of this village, Naim, is quite descriptive. It means "pleasant" or "pasture." Today it is a Moslem town.

Our sojourn in the village of Naim was short, but it did affect me deeply. One of the most touching episodes in the life of Jesus took place here. At the gate of the town Jesus restored life to the only son of a widow.

When we arrived we found some of the inhabitants shearing sheep right in the middle of a narrow street. It was also milking time and a herd of goats were gathered together waiting their turn to be milked by the women of the village.

We went directly to the Franciscan Chapel for the celebration of the Eucharist. The scriptural readings and the homily naturally centered on the miracle of Jesus raising to life this young man who had died. The chapel was built to commemorate this compassionate act of Jesus.

The Gospel account of this event according to St. Luke is quite brief, but we can read much between the lines. This episode brings to light the loving compassion of Jesus. Luke says: "As he [Jesus] approached the gate of the town a dead man was being carried out, the only son of a widowed mother" (*Luke 7:12*). These few words speak volumes.

According to the traditional beliefs of that day, not to have a male child to carry on the family name was considered a punishment from God. Luke tells us that the young man was "the only

97

son of a widowed mother." Since she was widowed there was no hope for a future son to preserve the family. Even if the mother remarried and was blessed with a son, he would continue a different family, the family of the father and husband. The sorrow of this mother was due not only to the loss of a child, but also to the realization that her family line was dying out. She foresaw the disgrace and rejection which would accompany his death.

Another dimension of the loving concern of Jesus surfaces here. Jesus was not yet in the town. He could not know the circumstances from a merely human point of view. He was not even asked to use His divine powers to remedy this tragic event. On two other occasions of raising a person to life, Jesus had been asked for His divine intervention; on this occasion Jesus Himself took the initiative. He reached out in loving concern for this poor mother. His unsolicited response reveals the immensity of the love of His Sacred Heart.

What profit we can reap from this touching event! We know that "Jesus Christ is the same yesterday, today and forever" (*Hebrews 13:8*). He is equally concerned about you and me. He comes to our need with the same tenderness and solicitude with which He approached the plight of the mother at Naim. He knew the heartache, the pain of separation of the widowed mother who lost both her husband and her son.

Jesus knows the joy and happiness which fills our hearts. He also knows the heartaches and the disappointment, the pain and frustrations which plague us. He responds with great love and compassion to our every need, whether it be physical, spiritual or psychological. All He asks is our faith and trust.

May your faith be deepened and your trust increased as you pray and listen to His Word during these next days.

Luke 7:11-17 — *"The Lord was moved with pity upon seeing her and said to her, 'Do not cry.'"*

Luke 8:40-56 — *"Fear is useless; what is needed is trust and her life will be spared."*

John 11:1-43 — *"... whoever is alive and believes in me will never die."*

Psalm 16:1-11 — *"... nor will you suffer your faithful one to undergo corruption."*

Romans 14:1-11 — *"... Christ died and came to life again, that he might be Lord of both the dead and the living."*

I Corinthians 15:35-58 — *"The trumpet will sound and the dead will be raised incorruptible. . . ."*

Philippians 1:12-26 — *"For, to me, 'life' means Christ; hence dying is so much gain."*

28. Jericho

"Unless the Lord guard the city,
in vain does the guard keep vigil"
(Psalm 127:1).

Jericho is rich in antiquity and is also noted for its recurring mention in the New Testament times. Its name, Jericho, means "the city of palms." This name is appropriate, for it is a delightful oasis with beautiful gardens of bananas, oranges and dates.

Jericho is first mentioned in the Bible when the Israelites arrived on the opposite shore of the Jordan River. This was the place designated by God for their crossing into the Promised Land. It was the first city which they captured as they began to take possession of the land of promise flowing with milk and honey.

However, by the time the Israelites arrived Jericho already had a long history of several thousands of years. Ancient Jericho dates back some 10,000 years. It is the oldest city in history to be excavated. Tell es Sultan marks the site of ancient Jericho. The rich archeological finds reveal much about the ancient culture and civilization which existed long before Jesus walked through this area.

Near the Tell we found the Fountain of Eliseus. The prophet Eliseus changed the bitterness of this source of water by casting a handful of salt into the water. It has produced refreshing water ever since (*II Kings 2:19*).

Jericho was always a stopping place for pilgrims on their way to Jerusalem for the Pasch. It is certain that Jesus stayed here as He came down from Galilee or from east of the Jordan. Its lush gardens and plentiful water supply made it a real mecca for

Jericho — ruins of a palace.

pilgrims. The Jericho which Jesus visited was the third Jericho, the one built by Herod.

Close to Jericho is an abandoned refugee camp which is a bleak reminder of man's inhumanity to man. This camp is made up of huts built out of clay and roofed with palm branches. Its haunting appearance speaks to us of the gruesome horrors of war.

There was so much to ponder here: the ancient Jericho rich in its archeological treasures, modern Jericho with its lush gardens, the Herodian Jericho which Jesus saw, and the deserted refugee camp. All this reminded me of God's loving care in spite of man's sinfulness.

The Father's loving concern for His people miraculously provided and protected the Israelites as they crossed the Jordan into the Promised Land. It was in this vicinity that Jesus proved His compassionate concern as He healed, encouraged and brought the Good News to these inhabitants. In our own day that same loving Father provided for all the victims of war who found food and a haven close to the life-giving waters which flow so freely in this oasis here in the Judean desert.

That same God is my Abba, loving and caring for me at every moment of the day. When I begin to recount His benefactions, it staggers my imagination. Such a reflection can bring a deep sense of gratitude.

May your recalling of some of these events in the Scriptures suggested here for your prayer bring you to an overwhelming appreciation of His goodness and also to a generous loving response to His love.

Joshua 5:10; 6:27 — " . . . to Joshua the Lord said, 'I have delivered Jericho and its king into your power.' "

Psalm 55:2-15 — "... for in the city I see violence and strife; day and night they prowl about upon its walls."

Matthew 20:29-34 — "As they were leaving Jericho ... two blind men ... began to shout, 'Lord, Son of David, have pity on us!' "

Mark 10:46-52 — "... there was a blind beggar Bartimaeus ... sitting by the roadside."

Luke 10:25-37 — "There was a man going down from Jerusalem to Jericho who fell prey to robbers."

Luke 19:1-10 — "Zacchaeus, hurry down. I mean to stay at your house today."

Hebrews 11:1-40 — "Because of Israel's faith, the walls of Jericho fell after being encircled for seven days."

29. Shrine of the Pater Noster

"Lord, teach us to pray ... "
(Luke 11:1).

High on the top of Mount Olivet, overlooking the city of Jerusalem on one side and the hills and desert of Judea on the other, is another sacred place. It is the Shrine of the Pater Noster (The Church of Our Father). It is very close to the place of the Ascension of Jesus into heaven. This place is venerated for many reasons.

It is the spot where Jesus explained to His apostles the fate which would overtake the Holy City (*Matthew 24:1-3*). For this reason the first chapel was called the Church of the Eleona.

Later when the Crusaders built a church here, they called it the Pater Noster Church because this also marks the spot where Jesus taught the Our Father to His apostles. Jesus often came to the Mount of Olives to spend time in prayer. Luke tells us that one day when He finished His prayer, the disciples asked Him to teach them how to pray. As you enter this shrine cared for by the Carmelites, you pass by the cloistered area to find the Lord's Prayer written in 60 different languages on large plaques on the wall. As you continue down this corridor, you will arrive at the very spot where Jesus was praying on the top of Mount Olivet which is commemorated as the place where He taught the Our Father to His disciples.

As you pass through the open courtyard, which is the unfinished nave of a basilica in honor of the Sacred Heart, you will find another cave. You enter this cave by going down 18 steps into a large grotto. The apostles were to have met here sometime later to approve the articles of faith which they had drawn up from the teachings of Jesus. This cave is supported by 12 semicircular columns which some believe suggested the 12 articles of the Creed which was confirmed here.

The open court is the beginning of the construction of a basilica here in honor of the Sacred Heart. It has never been finished. However, the raised floor of the sanctuary portion has been laid and the altar placed in the center. This forms an ideal open-air chapel. We had the privilege of offering Mass here on the last day of our sojourn in the

Land of the Holy One.

For all Christians the Lord's Prayer is one of the most popular formulas of prayer. Our present form is not scripturally exact, but it has been sanctioned by the passage of time. The Lord's Prayer as recorded in Luke has probably the original number of petitions, while Matthew added other sayings of Jesus. Later the doxology "for thine is the kingdom, the power and the glory forever" was added. This doxology is found in a second-century Christian manual called the *Didache*. Most of the phrases of the Our Father are also found in contemporary Jewish prayer.

As we prayed the Our Father in the Grotto of the Lord's Prayer, it really came alive for me. I could almost hear Jesus teaching this beautiful prayer, phrase by phrase, to His apostles. At the Eucharistic Liturgy later on we prayed the Our Father very slowly and meditatively. Ever since that day the Our Father has become more of an actual prayer for me rather than a mere formula of speaking to our loving Father.

In addition to listening to God speaking to you through these suggested scriptural texts, I would recommend that you pray the Lord's Prayer very slowly, pausing for a considerable time after each phrase and reflecting on its meaning. You may have a surprise awaiting you.

Luke 11:1-13 — "*. . . how much more will the heavenly Father give the Holy Spirit to those who ask him.*"

Matthew 24:1-14 — "*The man who holds out to the end, however, is the one who will see salvation.*"

Exodus 16:4-15 — "I will now rain down bread from heaven for you."

Psalm 2:1-11 — "The Lord said to me, 'You are my son. . . . ' "

Matthew 6:5-15 — "Whenever you pray, go to your room . . . and pray to your Father in private."

Matthew 6:25-34 — "Your heavenly Father knows all that you need."

Psalm 141:1-10 — "Let my prayer come like incense before you. . . . "

30. Tabor — Faith Confirmation

"North and south you created;
Tabor and Hermon rejoice at your name"
(Psalm 89:13).

Our prayer pilgrimage to Mount Tabor was one of those experiences which are virtually impossible to express in words. We travelled by bus to the foot of this holy mountain, then walked up to the summit. The road to the top is a steady and steep grade of hairpin curves and switchbacks. It is hemmed in on either side by lush vegetation of evergreen oaks, carol trees, terebinths and many other varieties whose names I did not learn. As we climbed higher and higher, more and more of the rich, fertile valley came into view. At this time of year we could see an expanse like a gorgeous green carpet stretching for miles.

Mount Tabor is a sugarloaf mountain soaring some 1500 feet above the valley floor. It stands alone in all its majestic beauty.

In order to appreciate more deeply the wonderful panorama which one can enjoy from the top of Mount Tabor, a person should do so with Sacred Scripture at his fingertips. Thus we can recall the heroic deeds, the mighty wars, the terrific manifestations of divine power which took place in this garden spot of Armageddon.

From the summit we could see Mount Hermon to the northeast, and to the south some of the mountains of Galilee: Little Hermon, Ebal, Gerizim and Gilboa. The enchanting plain of Esdraelon below was breathtaking, to say the least.

As I stood there in awe and wonder, the landscape helped me to understand more fully the background of the Sermon on the Mount and the parables of Jesus. I could also see the rich, fertile fields which were sanctified by His presence and where so many of His miracles were performed.

For good reason Jesus chose this mountain to manifest His divinity so magnificently in the Transfiguration. It seems to me that He not only sanctified this hallowed peak with His presence, but that He also left some of the radiance of His Transfiguration on this holy hill.

I reflected on how the Transfiguration was the second confirmation which we received from the Father. At the time of the Baptism of Jesus in the River Jordan, the voice of the Father was heard to say: "This is my beloved Son. My favor rests on him." Thus the Father confirmed and endorsed the teaching mission of Jesus. On Mount Tabor, again the Father's confirming voice was heard to say: "This is my Son, my Chosen One." Along with this came the admonition: "Listen to him" (*Luke 9:35*).

The Father's confirmation was timely because the faith of the three favorite apostles, Peter, James and John, needed to be supported as Jesus began His mission of rejection, suffering, and finally death. As the intrigue, hatred and plotting against Jesus grew in intensity, the apostles had to be assured that Jesus is God and that He was willingly laying down His life (*John 10:17f*). What appeared to be a miserable defeat was actually a tremendous triumph. Such are God's ways.

How good God is and how sensitive to our needs! Like the disciples, many times we, too, need confirmation of His loving concern for each one of us. We need to know of His love, which is such a forgiving, healing and redeeming love. Constantly we must be reminded that God is present to us at all times.

These are the truths which Jesus taught right here in this very area of Mount Tabor. The Father's confirmation gives validity to these teachings and reassurances to our weak faith.

I experienced a deepening of my own faith as I tarried on this great mountain. As we listen to His Word may our faith be strengthened and enriched.

Luke 9:28-46 — *"While he was praying, his face changed in appearance and his clothes became dazzlingly white."*

Matthew 3:13-17 — *"This is my beloved Son. My favor rests on him."*

Exodus 19:9-25 — *"I am coming to you in a dense cloud. . . ."*

Psalm 89:2-19 — *"North and south you created; Tabor and Hermon rejoice at your name."*

Romans 8:14-25 — *"And hoping for what we cannot see means awaiting it with patient endurance."*

Exodus 34:29-35 — *". . . the skin of his face had become radiant while he conversed with the Lord."*

John 1:1-18 — *"No one has ever seen God. It is God the only Son . . . who has revealed him."*

31. Tabor — Transfiguration in the Eucharist

"Lord, how good that we are here!"
(Matthew 17:4).

It was almost noon when we arrived at the summit of Mount Tabor. The Franciscan Sisters served us a delicious lunch in the pilgrim house. After that we went over to the basilica for a time of prayer and also to celebrate the Eucharistic Liturgy.

The Church of the Transfiguration is built over the site where Jesus supposedly was transfigured before His favorite apostles, Peter, James and John. A wide stairway of 12 steps leads down into the crypt where the ancient walls and an ancient altar were uncovered in the excavations. In this crypt are represented the symbols of the life of Jesus:

His Birth, His Presence in the Eucharist, His Transfiguration and also His Death and Resurrection. These mosaics depict artistically the story of His ministry.

As we prepared for the Mass, a Franciscan Brother was most hospitable and helpful. It was my privilege to celebrate Mass on this ancient altar which theologically is the spot where Jesus was transfigured and where Peter suggested three tabernacles should be built, one for Moses, one for Elijah and one for Jesus.

The Eucharist Celebration was a very joyous and happy occasion for all of us. The Liturgy of the Word told again the magnificent story of what took place here. The theme of the Mass and the homily reminded us that Jesus is constantly transfigured in our own lives. Each day as He is born again on our altars His presence is renewed within us. As we strive to open ourselves constantly to the influence of His divine life, He becomes more present to us.

This thought was brought home to me very forcefully in the third Eucharistic prayer. We pray that these gifts may, through the power of the Holy Spirit, really become the body and blood of Christ for us. The experiential awareness of the presence of Jesus in the Eucharist is a special grace from God. This awareness can be for us a minor transfiguration.

Jesus became alive and real for me during our Mass. All my friends offering the Mass with me seemed to have had the same experience.

After Mass I wanted to be alone. On that mountain the Father had admonished us in these words: "Listen to Him!" I wanted to listen to Him. I wanted to hear Him at the very depth of my being. I did not want anyone to disturb my rendezvous with Jesus. That's why I escaped and went into the garden. No, I was not alone on that narrow trail; the presence of Jesus was very real to me.

I saw the beauty of His creation in the luscious landscape as far as I could see. I saw His beauty in the azure blue vault of heaven, which was dotted with beautiful fleecy clouds here and there. I felt His presence in the trees, the brilliant carpet of wild flowers stretching in every direction. I felt His strength in the huge rocks and boulders which seemed to support the mountains so firmly.

I wanted to dance and sing. I wanted to hop and skip down the narrow path. Jesus is alive! He is with me always! I prayed that I might have an occasional transfiguration in my life to sustain my weak faith.

We need to remind ourselves that Jesus is always faithful and He did promise: "I will not leave you orphaned; I will come back to you" (*John 14:18*).

The following Scripture passages recommended for your prayer will help make this truth more real to you.

Matthew 17:1-8 — *"He was transfigured before their eyes."*

Exodus 33:7-23 — *"I will make all my beauty pass before you. . . ."*

Psalm 2:1-11 — *"You are my son; this day I have begotten you."*

Isaiah 42:1-9 — *"Here is my servant whom I uphold, my chosen one with whom I am pleased. . . ."*

Deuteronomy 18:15-22 — *"A prophet like me will the Lord, your God, raise up. . . ."*

111

II Peter 1:12-19 — ". . . we were eyewitnesses of his sovereign majesty."

Psalm 97:1-12 — "Be glad in the Lord, you just, and give thanks to his holy name."

32. Tabor — Vestibule of Heaven

"Extol the Lord, our God, and worship at his holy mountain . . . " (Psalm 99:9).

Mount Tabor's graceful form rising above the valley, its picturesque site, its verdant vegetation and the exquisite splendor of its panoramic view make it one of the most beautiful mountains in Israel. It is not surprising to hear the psalmist calling upon the mountains to witness to the glory of God: "North and south you created; Tabor and Hermon rejoice at your name" (*Psalm 89:13*).

Guerin described this beautiful mountain in these words: "Tabor rises up to heaven like an altar in the greatest sanctuary of the world."

The time for us to leave Mount Tabor came all too soon. I wanted to walk down the trail to be alone with my thoughts. No, I was not alone; Jesus was very present to me.

The path was even more beautiful than the roadway by which we had climbed to the top. I paused many times to let my eyes feast on the enchanting beauty of spring bursting forth in the whole Plain of Esdraelon. Along the pathway the fragrance of the blossoms filled the air. Occasionally I could see a shepherd on the mountainside keeping a watchful eye on his sheep and goats. How easily my thoughts turned to Jesus, the Good Shepherd, and how carefully He guards our every footstep!

Another dimension of the Transfiguration started to unfold itself in my reflections. Jesus permitted His divinity to radiate through His human body in order to strengthen our faith, especially in times of distress and suffering. He also wanted to give us the assurance of His abiding presence with us at all times, but especially in the Eucharistic Celebration when He renews His presence under the humble forms of bread and wine.

Jesus had still another reason for this divine manifestation on the top of Tabor. We can so easily become earthbound. Our vision can be so myopic. We can be so engrossed in the mundane aspects of everyday living that we lose sight of our final destiny.

Mount Tabor revealed a heavenly mystery. While living among us Jesus had often spoken about the Kingdom and His second coming. In order to remove any doubt about the kind of kingdom He came to establish, and also to confirm our faith in what lies ahead of us before we reach that Kingdom, He gave us on Mount Tabor a wonderful vision of His glory and a foreshadowing of the glory of the Kingdom awaiting us.

Jesus wants to awaken within us a yearning for that heavenly vision. He came to renew our spiritual nature and transform us into His own likeness by making us sharers in His Godhead.

Jesus invites us to climb to the top of the mountain with Him each day. His invitation is not to climb a mountain in the literal sense, but rather to raise our minds and hearts to those realms where His presence and His glory become more apparent to us. This may be on a retreat or during our daily hour of prayer, or as we spend our day in the desert, or even while we pause in our daily routine.

From such a height Jesus can more easily reveal His abiding presence. From the height of a mountain we can better see beyond the confines of our own narrow little world, in order to comprehend more fully God's divine designs in our life.

With this vision we can more easily keep God as the number one priority in our lives. Then God, in turn, will grant us occasional minor transfigurations.

Let us listen to the gentle voice of God calling us to the summit of the mountain and on to the celestial glory of our home with Him.

Mark 9:2-8 — "... *Jesus took Peter, James, and John off by themselves with him and led them up a high mountain."*

I Kings 19:9-18 — "*After the fire there was a tiny whispering sound."*

Philippians 3:17-21 — "*He will give a new form to this lowly body of ours. . . . "*

Psalm 99:1-9 — "*Extol the Lord, our God, and worship at his holy mountain. . . . "*

II Corinthians 3:4-18 — "*All of us, gazing on the Lord's glory . . . are being transformed from glory to glory. . . . "*

Luke 24:25-35 — "*How slow you are to believe all that the prophets have announced!"*

Revelation 21:9-27 — "*It gleamed with the splendor of God."*

33. Bethany

" . . . one thing only is required.
Mary has chosen the better portion
and she shall not be deprived of it"
(Luke 10:42).

The name "Bethany" awakens in us many happy memories. I looked forward to our visit to this village to which Jesus frequently went and where He found a haven of love and acceptance. Bethany is located on the eastern slope of Mount Olivet about two miles distant from Jerusalem. Lazarus and his two sisters, Martha and Mary, lived here. Jesus loved them dearly and He knew He was always welcome in their home.

When Jesus came to Jerusalem, He probably stayed with Martha, Mary and Lazarus. Toward the end of His earthly life it was not safe for Him to remain in the Holy City because of the hatred and plotting of the Pharisees. As far as we know He spent His last night on earth in the home of these special friends.

The former village of Bethany is located in an olive grove near the tomb of Lazarus. It was excavated at one time, but the home of Lazarus and his two sisters was not found, nor was the home of Simon the Leper, with whom Jesus dined.

Today the Church of St. Lazarus rises above the place where Lazarus was buried for four days before Jesus miraculously restored him to life. The church is rather severe in aspect. It is a dull gray. The interior is brightened by three large mosaics which depict the scene of the resurrection of Lazarus, the meeting of Jesus with Mary and Martha, and the anointing of Jesus in the house of Simon the Leper.

A mosque has been built next to the church, so

it is impossible to enter the tomb from within the church. As you leave the courtyard of the church you will find a stairway leading down to the grave. You can descend by 24 well-worn steps which will bring you to an antechamber and then to the tomb of Lazarus. A rectangular slab of stone which covered the opening of the tomb can still be seen. This coincides with what John tells us: "It was a cave with a stone laid across it" (*John 11:38*).

Neither the area where the village of Bethany was once located nor the Church of St. Lazarus is very impressive or inspirational. However, recalling the touching events which took place here makes this a treasured spot.

Lazarus and his sisters were delighted to welcome Jesus and have Him stay with them. On one occasion Martha, in typically oriental style, was preparing an elegant meal for Jesus and His disciples. Jesus and His disciples, on the other hand, had been accustomed to living a very frugal life and such preparation was not expected. When Martha complained about Mary's lack of cooperation in preparing the meal, Jesus used the occasion to chide Martha ever so gently. He explained that nourishment for the soul was even more important; hence He lauded Mary, the mystic, who had chosen the better part. All that Jesus intended to emphasize was that our priorities must be in the right order. He was not depreciating domestic work.

There is a lesson for us in this event. Mary had laid everything aside to give her undivided attention to Jesus. She devoted herself completely to Him and had eyes and ears for Him alone. Her focus was ever fixed on Jesus and what He was saying.

Jesus seeks a "Bethany" in our midst where He might find a genuine welcome and where He might reveal Himself and His great love for us. He wants loving acceptance. He asks us to empty our hearts of everything which will not lead us to a closer friendship and union with Him. He wants to shower His love and attention upon us. At times we permit various attachments to prevent us from being totally receptive to Him. He bids us, "Live on in me, as I do in you . . . " (*John 15:4*).

Our prayer time of listening will make us more receptive and will draw us into a deeper union with Him. Lord, teach us to listen not only with our ears but with our whole being as You speak to us through Your Word.

John 11:1-44 — "*I am the resurrection and the life. . . .*"

Luke 10:38-42 — "*Mary has chosen the better portion and she shall not be deprived of it.*"

I Timothy 6:1-21 — "*Charge them to do good, to be rich in good works and generous, sharing what they have.*"

Matthew 17:22-28 — "*The Son of Man . . . will be raised up on the third day.*"

Romans 14:1-11 — "*. . . Christ died and came to life again, that he might be lord of both the dead and the living.*"

John 12:1-11 — "*. . . she anointed Jesus' feet. Then she dried his feet with her hair. . . .*"

Psalm 27:1-14 — "*One thing I ask of the Lord . . . That I may gaze on the loveliness of the Lord. . . .*"

34. Dominus Flevit

*"Coming within sight of the city,
he wept over it . . . " (Luke 19:41).*

On a bright, balmy spring morning we walked up the Mount of Olives to a place overlooking the Garden of Olives and the city of Jerusalem situated on the next hill. This is the spot where Jesus stopped, looked over the Holy City and wept bitter tears. This incident is enshrined here in a new and imposing church called the Dominus Flevit Church (The Lord Wept). The outside view of the church gives the impression of an elegant lookout tower with a cupola and four pillars at the corner of the building and extending a little beyond the roof. The shrine is a work of art.

Inside the church is a large picture window above the altar table which looks across the whole Kidron Valley with a commanding view of Jerusalem. We had the privilege of offering Mass on this altar on Palm Sunday, the very day that Jesus wept over the city. This panoramic window brought into the congregation the whole city of Jerusalem.

I sat quietly for a time and became enthralled by the view of the Holy City. I tried to call to mind the indescribable spectacle which must have met the eyes of Jesus that beautiful morning. It was spring and the sun was climbing behind Mount Olivet into a crystal-clear sky. The sun bathed the city on the opposite hill with all its glistening splendor. The towers of Mount Sion must have glowed with their shining white marble. In the foreground the Temple in all its radiance, with its golden dome, its bronze doors, its marble columns

Jerusalem — the Temple Mount framed by the grill of Dominus Flevit Church.

and towers glistening in the rising sun, rose majestically above the Kidron Valley.

Jesus saw all this, but at the sight could no longer contain Himself. He wept. He lamented the disastrous fate which awaited the Holy City. He could see the Roman legions marching from the north, murdering His people and decimating the Holy City so that not one stone remained upon another. As He paused to view the city and as He wept, He spoke words of touching compassion for that stiff-necked and blind people who refused the salvation He had offered them.

Here we see, once again, the great love overflowing the heart of Jesus. He wept not because He was soon to be cruelly mocked, tortured and executed like a criminal, but because the people He loved would soon be annihilated. He offered them His Kingdom with the challenge, "reform your lives and believe in the gospel" and "follow me!" Jesus was sad and deeply grieved because they would not accept that challenge.

As I sat there in this beautiful church, viewing through this picture window modern Jerusalem with its huge Dome of the Rock now replacing the Temple, I wondered how many cities Jesus must be weeping over at the present time. I was thinking not only of those large metropolitan cities which are often called "sin city," but I was thinking also of all those cities in which people are turning a deaf ear to His voiceless voice speaking within them. I thought of those inhabitants who are too indifferent to give Him a passing thought, or those who are too attached to the material standards of this world and too engrossed in amassing a comfortable fortune to be bothered with "wasting time" with the Lord.

I prayed for the city I call home. I prayed for the city you call home. I prayed for all the cities of the entire world which are home to any one of God's creatures.

As you listen to His Word, perhaps you may discover that He may be weeping over something in your life. Perhaps you may weep with Jesus so that your tears may draw many souls to Him.

Luke 19:41-44 — *"Coming within sight of the city, he wept over it. . . . "*

Psalm 137:1-9 — *"By the streams of Babylon we sat and wept when we remembered Zion."*

Matthew 23:36-39 — *"How often have I yearned to gather your children, as a mother bird gathers her young under her wings, but you refused me."*

Lamentations 2:13-19 — *"Let your tears flow like a torrent day and night. . . . "*

Ecclesiastes 3:1-8 — *"There is . . . A time to weep, and a time to laugh. . . . "*

Job 16:1-22 — *"My face is inflamed with weeping. . . . "*

Psalm 42:2-12 — *"My tears are my food day and night, as they say to me day after day, 'Where is your God?'"*

35. Bethphage

*"This people pays me lip service
but their heart is far from me"
(Matthew 15:8).*

On the morning of Palm Sunday we walked up the Mount of Olives to celebrate the Eucharistic Liturgy in the Dominus Flevit Church. This church marks the spot where Jesus wept over the city of Jerusalem. After Mass we continued up the Mount of Olives to the village of Bethphage. This village is important for two reasons. In the first place, it is where Martha and Mary went out to meet Jesus when He came to restore Lazarus to life (*John 11:29*). Secondly, this is the village to which Jesus sent His disciples to obtain a donkey for His triumphant entry into Jerusalem (*Luke 19:29*).

A church was built in this village to commemorate these two important events in the life of Jesus. Today one can see the paintings in the church which recall these episodes. In the Franciscan garden one can also find tombs which were sealed by rolling a round stone over the entrance of the grave.

For many centuries the Palm Sunday procession has begun at this church and proceeded down the slope of Mount Olivet into Jerusalem through St. Stephen's gate.

On Palm Sunday we went over to Bethphage to spend some time in prayer and reflection on the events which took place here. We sat together in the garden. We could hear all the noises of the people busy about many things. We attracted the attention of little children who watched us curiously and begged for alms. All this was a distraction until I began to think that this was precisely what happened when Jesus came to this village where He

122

mounted the donkey to continue His journey into Jerusalem.

Our own group went over the route of the triumphal procession on Palm Sunday. We sang, prayed and remained in silence as we journeyed along. It was a moving experience. Later that afternoon some of us returned to Bethphage to walk in the big annual Palm Sunday procession. It took many hours to begin the procession and also to reach our destination. As we walked along in the procession with thousands of onlookers lining the route, my thoughts and imagination frequently turned back to what might have occurred to Jesus as He traversed this same route. I wonder what thoughts filled His mind, what sorrow filled His heart because He realized that many were not sincere in welcoming Him, while others hated Him.

As we proceeded, the police and military were very much in evidence. With stoic faces they watched the proceedings and I detected some cynical glances. I was reminded of the disapproving Pharisees trying to quiet the people and disband that huge procession which formed to accompany Jesus into the Holy City.

On the day after His triumphal entry Jesus passed this way again. He cursed the fig tree which had leaves but no fruit (*Mark 11:12*). Jesus was trying to show His disciples how fruitless were the events of the day before. He had been offered the show of a deceptive welcome, a welcome which bore no fruit. Two great prophets of the Old Testament used similar symbolic acts to impress the people: Jeremiah broke the potter's vessel and Ezekiel shaved off his beard with a sword.

Recalling all these events gave me reason to pause and reflect on my own response to the entry of Jesus into my life. Am I receptive to all that He wants to do in my life or do I cling to my own plans, projects and self-will?

In your prayer, live these events with Jesus and the prophets and permit your heart to respond.

Matthew 21:1-11 — *"Blessed is he who comes in the name of the Lord."*

John 11:17-43 — *"When Mary came to the place where Jesus was, seeing him, she fell at his feet. . . . "*

Luke 19:28-40 — *"If they were to keep silence, I tell you the very stones would cry out."*

Mark 11:12-26 — *"Never again shall anyone eat of your fruit!"*

Psalm 5:1-13 — *"For in their mouth there is no sincerity; their heart teems with treacheries."*

Jeremiah 19:1-15 — *"And you shall break the flask in the sight of the men who went with you. . . . "*

Ezekiel 5:1-15 — *" . . . take a sharp sword and use it like a barber's razor, passing it over your head and beard."*

36. The Banquet in the Upper Room

*"He rained manna upon them for food
and gave them heavenly bread"
(Psalm 78:24).*

With a feeling of excitement and expectancy we set out to visit the Upper Room, or Cenacle. As we approached the site, we entered a courtyard to find a stairway leading to the Upper Room. Over the years so many pilgrims have climbed those stairs that they have caused deep depressions to be worn into their treads.

As we entered the Cenacle we discovered a large room approximately 30 by 45 feet, completely devoid of any furnishings. Three gothic windows furnish the only light in the room. There is no artificial light. The room is divided into two naves separated by columns supporting several arches. In this bare room is venerated the memory of the institution of two very important Sacraments: the Holy Eucharist and the Priesthood of the New Covenant.

The Upper Room is in a complex of other rooms. On the first-floor level there are two rooms. One is dedicated to the washing of the feet, which took place before the institution of the Holy Eucharist. The other room is supposedly the room in which Jesus appeared to His disciples on the day of the Resurrection.

From the Cenacle a flight of eight steps leads into a room in which is venerated the Descent of the Holy Spirit on Pentecost Sunday.

My first visit to the Cenacle was somewhat of a disappointment. The Jews, who own the building, will not permit any Christian services to be held here. I had long anticipated the great privilege of celebrating the Eucharist in the very spot where Jesus gave us the gift of Himself in the Eucharist.

My second disappointment was of a lesser calibre. A large number of people were making a pilgrimage here. The noise was deafening and the confusion catastrophic.

I tried to find a corner where I might be alone with my own thoughts. At first I attempted to visualize the setting of the Last Supper. How was the room arranged? Where did Jesus recline? I considered many other little factors of no consequence whatever. My thoughts then turned to what had taken place here. More important by far is the mystery of love which had been demonstrated here. Jesus gave us His divine life cached under the appearances of bread and wine as food for our pilgrimage back to the Father.

During my journey into the Sinai Desert I had experienced how God had been the only source of hope for the Israelites in the desert. I had experienced the absolute impossibility of survival without God. The manna was the only food on which the Israelites could survive. Without it they were doomed to starvation. They could never have reached the Promised Land.

The Old Testament not only prepares us for the New Testament, but it also finds its fulfillment in the New Covenant. Just as God sustained and nourished His people on their long journey to the Promised Land, so Jesus provides for our spiritual nourishment along our journey in this land of sojourn. He pours His divine life into us and renews and implements that life daily at the Eucharistic Celebration.

Each day Jesus invites us: "Come to me, all you who are weary and find life burdensome, and I will refresh you" (*Matthew 11:28*).

May our prayer time this week bring us to a

deeper realization and appreciation of this magnificent gift to us.

Luke 22:7-20 — *"I have greatly desired to eat this Passover with you before I suffer."*

Exodus 16:4-15 — *"This is the bread which the Lord has given you to eat."*

John 6:35-51 — *"I myself am the bread of life."*

John 13:1-17 — *"Do you understand what I just did for you?"*

John 6:52-58 — *". . . if you do not eat the flesh of the Son of Man and drink his blood, you have no life in you."*

I Corinthians 11:23-29 — *"A man should examine himself first; only then should he eat of the bread and drink of the cup."*

Acts 1:1-14 — *"Together they devoted themselves to constant prayer."*

37. The Cenacle
and the Eucharistic Sacrifice

*"Through him
let us continually offer God
a sacrifice of praise . . . " (Hebrews 13:15).*

We returned to the Cenacle on Holy Thursday evening. It was already dark when we arrived and there were no lights in the Upper Room. We gathered there to spend some time in prayer. With the aid of a flashlight we read and contemplated the Gospel account of the institution of the Holy Eucharist, and also parts of the Last Discourse of Jesus to His apostles, which had taken place here in this Upper Room. It was a precious time indeed. The darkness was conducive to prayer. An added touch to an atmosphere of prayer was the faint moonlight filtering through the gothic windows.

I wish I could convey to you the peace and joy which flooded my soul as I pondered the great love Jesus has for each one of us, and how that love prompted Him to remain eucharistically among us. As I listened to the words which Jesus was addressing to His apostles on that first Holy Thursday evening, I could also visualize Him rising majestically above all the hatred, intrigue and plotting which was ensnaring Him more and more like a noose. Jesus knew that His hour was rapidly approaching; yet He was not thinking of Himself. On the contrary, His final teaching was an encouragement and consolation to His apostles because He was promising them His continued presence through the outpouring of His Holy Spirit upon them.

After our prayer time we wanted to follow Jesus not only in our prayer, but literally. We walked down a street with stone steps which are said to have existed since the time of Jesus. This street was very likely the same route which Jesus took on His way to the garden. We next crossed the Brook Kidron and entered the Garden of Gethsemane. Like Jesus and His chosen friends we sang and prayed as we journeyed along. It was a balmy spring evening with a full moon shimmering its rays on our path.

On this memorable evening another aspect of the Holy Eucharist kept returning to my mind. The Eucharist is also a sacrifice. Jesus began that sacrifice in the Cenacle when He made the complete and total oblation of Himself to the Father for our redemption. This oblation was to reach its climax the next day when He poured out in immolation His last drop of blood from His pierced side on Calvary's hill.

At the Last Supper Jesus began that sacrifice. He continued that oblation as He journeyed into the Garden of Olives, where He was betrayed, arrested and ridiculously condemned to death. The entire passion and death was a continuation of the sacrificial gift of Himself to the Father in our name.

Today Jesus comes to us in the Eucharistic Celebration and mystically re-enacts this drama of oblation and immolation with us and for us. For "with him, and through him, and in him" we can offer all praise, honor and glory to the Father.

Our purpose in life is to give ourselves, and all that we do, to the Father. We really do not have an effective means of presenting ourselves to the Father except through Jesus. Furthermore, the gift of ourselves is often self-centered and half-hearted and certainly not worthy of God. For this precise reason Jesus invites us to bring to the altar our gift which is represented by the bread and wine. There He unites Himself with our token gift, and together we can give ourselves to the Father through Jesus. Thus our gift takes on an infinite dimension. What an astounding privilege is ours!

As I sat under an olive tree during the hours of that memorable night, with the moonlight filtering through the fresh green leaves of spring, I was simply overwhelmed with this mystery of God's love. All I could do was to respond in an almost inaudible whisper which came from the depth of my being: "Thank You, Jesus."

Let us relive that mystery as we pray during these next few days.

Matthew 26:17-30 — "... *this is my blood, the blood of the covenant, to be poured out in behalf of many for the forgiveness of sins.*"

John 10:10-18 — "... *the good shepherd lays down his life for the sheep.*"

Hebrews 10:1-18 — "... *we have been sanctified through the offering of the body of Jesus Christ once for all.*"

I Peter 2:1-10 — "*You, however, are a 'chosen race, a royal priesthood. . . .'*"

John 12:23-28 — "... *unless the grain of wheat falls to earth and dies, it remains just a grain of wheat.*"

Hebrews 9:11-15 — "... *how much more will the blood of Christ . . . cleanse our consciences from dead works to worship the Living God!*"

Acts 2:42-47 — "*They devoted themselves . . . to the breaking of bread. . . .*"

38. Cenacle to Gethsemane

*"Then he went out and made his way,
as was his custom,
to the Mount of Olives . . . "
(Luke 22:39).*

Holy Thursday is always a very special day in my life. However, its significance mounted far beyond my wildest expectations when I was privileged to pray with the Risen Jesus in the very area where the events of the first Holy Thursday took place.

On Holy Thursday evening we went to the Cenacle where Jesus instituted the Sacrament of His love. During our prayer vigil we shared and prayed together, especially with the words which Jesus spoke to us at the Last Supper (*John 14-17*).

It was quite dark since the Upper Room is not equipped with any artificial light. A flickering candle lapping away at the dark helped create a quieting, prayerful atmosphere. Again we had a sense of His presence among us in this hallowed spot.

After our time spent in prayer, we joined Jesus and His apostles. "After singing songs of praise, they walked out to the Mount of Olives" (*Mark 14:26*). We tried to follow the same path which Jesus had used on that tragic night. We walked down an ancient street and down some steps which were probably there in Jesus' day; they were possibly the very ones He used. Several times we paused to remain silent and reflect on what Jesus must have felt as He walked down this pathway and to think about the words He might have addressed to His apostles. I am sure that they were words of concern for them and not words of self-pity.

We prayed and sang as we walked along. A young Jewish couple followed us. When we stopped to talk to them, they remarked: "You must be American Christians because you pray so joyously and seem to be so happy."

After we crossed the Brook Kidron we entered the Garden of Olives. We nestled under an olive tree to spend another hour in company with Jesus living with us and within us. As we were settling into prayer the full moon of spring, in all its nocturnal splendor, looked down upon us through the leafy filigree of olive leaves. A soft breeze rustled the leaves gently, lending their hushed voices to our prayer.

Again we began our prayer by reading the evangelist's account of the dreadful agony which Jesus had suffered in this place. As our prayer became more and more quiet, there seemed to be a peaceful presence in our midst. During our prayer time there were long, silent pauses, as when heart speaks to heart. I had a feeling that Jesus was happy to have us accompany Him and relive with Him the experience of His total submission to the will of His Father.

As we recalled the terrible agony, the apparent indifference of His friends, the destructive forces of hatred and intrigue closing in upon Him, the seeming futility of it all, we saw that there could have been cause for fear, anger, discouragement and even despair. However, in Jesus and in us there was a deep inner peace rising above all these forces of evil. It was a peace which could not be verbalized.

Jesus had come to do the will of His Father. After the momentary shock, He could honestly and sincerely say, "Abba . . . let it be done as you would have it, not I" (*Mark 14:36*). It is this total act of submission to a loving Abba's will which is the only source of that quiet, interior peace which the world cannot give.

I heard myself saying to Jesus: "When the moment of my agony comes, when I am threatened on all sides, when I am helpless and discouraged, then teach me to say with all the sincerity of my whole being, Father, 'not my will, but yours be done' (*Luke 22:42*). Jesus, at that moment, I will count upon Your strength, for without You I can do nothing."

May our meeting Jesus in His Word each day help us to develop and maintain that attitude of total gift of self to our loving Abba. This is what discipleship is all about.

Mark 14:32-42 — "*Be on guard and pray that you may not be put to the test.*"

Luke 22:39-46 — "*In his anguish he prayed with all the greater intensity, and his sweat became like drops of blood falling to the ground.*"

Psalm 107:1-22 — "*And he led them forth from darkness and gloom and broke their bonds asunder.*"

Matthew 26:30-46 — "*The hour is on us when the Son of Man is to be handed over to the power of evil men.*"

II Samuel 16:5-14 — "*He threw stones at David and at all the King's officers. . . . *"

John 18:1-14 — "*Jesus, aware of all that would happen to him, stepped forward and said to them, 'Who is it you want?'* "

Psalm 3:1-9 — "When I lie down in sleep, I wake again, for the Lord sustains me. I fear not the myriads of people arrayed against me on every side."

39. Garden of Gethsemane

"Father, if it is your will,
take this cup from me; yet not my will
but yours be done" (Luke 22:42).

Frequently Jesus went to the Mount of Olives to spend time in prayer and also to rest for the night under the starry vault of heaven. His favorite spot was the olive groves in the Garden of Gethsemane.

I found myself being drawn back many times to the Garden of Gethsemane. It is a prayerful spot away from much of the noise and activity of the city. It is also within easy walking distance.

Here in the garden are eight ancient olive trees. No one can tell their exact age, but botanists claim that they may be 3000 years old. "The olive tree does not die" (Pliny), but continues to send out new shoots. It is possible that Jesus spent time under these trees and that they may have witnessed His prayer and agony. In addition to these old trees, there are many orchards of younger olive trees adjoining the garden.

A modern basilica was erected here as a gift

Jerusalem — the Garden of Gethsemane on the slopes of the Mount of Olives.

from many different countries. For this reason it is called the Church of All Nations as well as the Basilica of the Agony. In the sanctuary area before the main altar is a huge rock which is called the Rock of the Agony. Jesus could have knelt at this rock as He suffered that dreadful ordeal.

Here was a life-and-death struggle. Jesus, weak and gentle as a lamb attacked by a ravenous beast, nevertheless fought like a lion against the principalities and powers of darkness, even to the extreme of sweating blood. Haematidronis, or the sweating of blood, is not unknown in medical history. It is the result of terrible fear.

The words which Jesus prayed during that terrible struggle revealed His heart. The words of Jesus were not words of mistrust or anger or rebellion against God, but rather were deeply moving words in response to all the torment that the Father let Him undergo. What a mystery of childlike trust we find in the words of Jesus: "My Father, if it is possible, let this cup pass me by. Still, let it be as you would have it, not as I" (*Matthew 26:39*).

The windows of the basilica are alabaster, which is translucent but not transparent. These give a dim light at all times in the body of the church. The vaulted ceiling flickers with tiny stars. All this creates a nocturnal image and makes the Gospel account of the Agony more realistic, which in turn contributes much to an atmosphere of prayerfulness. Several times I spent the afternoon hours in prayer and found myself transported immediately by the semidarkness into the atmosphere of that first Holy Thursday night.

Each time I was drawn to return to the garden for prayer, I heard the same message re-echoing in my heart. I could hear the invitation of Jesus repeated several times to His apostles, "Remain here and stay awake with me . . . ," and then that pain-filled but gentle reproach: "So you could not stay awake with me for even an hour?" (*Matthew 26:38ff*). This same invitation to pray with Him for an hour is extended to me daily. I spent some time asking myself how generous my response has been to this oft-repeated invitation.

Jesus invites us to pray so that when there is agony in our life we might be able to say with Him, "Father . . . Your will be done." Even Jesus had to spend time alone in prayer before He was able to say "yes" to the Father. St. Luke says: "In his anguish he prayed with all the greater intensity" (*Luke 22:44*).

Our time spent in prayer will prepare, strengthen and enable us to say our "yes" to a loving Father who asks nothing of us which is not for our own welfare. In prayer we will hear and understand what the Father means when He says: "For I know well the plans I have in mind for you . . . plans for your welfare, not for woe!" (*Jeremiah 29:11*).

Luke 22:39-46 — "*Pray that you may not be put to the test.*"

Jeremiah 29:11-14 — "*For I know well the plans I have in mind for you. . . .*"

Matthew 26:36-46 — "*Then Jesus went with them to a place called Gethsemane.*"

Isaiah 63:1-6 — "*The wine press I have trodden alone. . . .*"

Psalm 25:1-22 — "*. . . my God. In you I trust; . . . let not my enemies exult over me.*"

Mark 14:32-42 — "*Take this cup away from me. But let it be as you would have it. . . .*"

40. The Grotto of Betrayal

". . . those whom I loved have turned against me!" (Job 19:19).

One of the monuments which has retained its primitive form since the time of Jesus is the Grotto of Betrayal. The grotto itself is an irregularly shaped cove situated at the foot of the Mount of Olives, a short distance from the Church of All Nations. It looks like a huge cave hewn out of rock. The bare roof and the rugged walls have been preserved intact. In approximately the twelfth century, the walls were adorned with paintings and the floor covered with mosaics which can scarcely be traced today. There has been no effort made to preserve these decorations since many wish to retain the cave as it originally was in the time of Jesus.

Jesus spent many nights in this garden and in this cave. He would teach all day in the Holy City and then would retire at night with His apostles to the cave to pray and rest for the next day. St. Luke tells us about the last days of the Divine Master's sojourn on earth: "He would teach in the temple by day and leave the city to spend the night on the Mount of Olives" (*Luke 21:37*).

On that memorable and tragic Holy Thursday evening Jesus came, as was His custom, to this place of prayer and rest. His favorite spot was well known to Judas, who would soon lead the temple guard to Jesus. John says: "The place was familiar to Judas as well (the one who was to hand him over) because Jesus had often met there with his disciples" (*John 18:2*).

The grotto has three altars with a fresco above each. The central altar is surmounted by "Jesus Praying With His Apostles." The altar on the right depicts the Kiss of Judas. The altar on the left has a fresco of the Assumption, since the death and Assumption of our Blessed Mother is believed to have taken place just a short distance away.

It was our privilege to offer the Holy Sacrifice of the Mass in this grotto during Holy Week. As we were about to begin, a group of pilgrims from Mexico arrived with their priest to join us at Mass. We had two homilies, one in Spanish and the other in English. These pilgrims from Mexico were warm and friendly, and we were grateful that they were able to join us in the Liturgy.

After Mass they greeted us profusely, embracing us with genuine Christian love. I thought immediately of the embrace and kiss of Judas. But how different and how tragic Judas' greeting had been! Yet if it had not been for the kiss of Judas, we would not have been able to extend Christian love to these wonderful people from Mexico, or to one another.

During the Mass, we were reminded in the homily that Judas was specially chosen to be one of the close and intimate friends of Jesus. What had gone wrong? Judas had lost his focus. His priorities had changed. Because of his preoccupation with material things and because of his inordinate attachment to money, Judas failed to keep his eyes ever fixed on Jesus. In fact, he intended to use Jesus for his own warped purposes. I am sure that

Judas never dreamed that Jesus would be taken prisoner. On previous occasions Jesus had escaped His enemies. I believe that Judas thought Jesus would do the same again and that he would be 30 pieces of silver the wealthier for it.

This reflection gave me reason to pause with some misgivings. I must frequently examine my own priorities. It is so easy to lose a sense of the one and all-important priority in my life. For example, it is easy for me to excuse myself from prayer on some days because I am too busy, even though I always make sure I have enough time to eat my meals regularly.

As we meet Jesus in our prayer each day our focus will more easily remain fixed on our first and foremost priority: God!

Matthew 26:6-16 — *"What are you willing to give me if I hand him over to you?"*

Luke 22:21-30 — *" . . . the hand of my betrayer is with me at this table."*

John 6:60-71 — *"Yet among you there are some who do not believe."*

Psalm 55:2-24 — *"If an enemy had reviled me, I could have borne it; . . . But you, my other self, my companion. . . . "*

Psalm 44:1-27 — *"You marked us out as sheep to be slaughtered; . . . You sold your people for no great price. . . . "*

Isaiah 63:1-6 — *"I looked about, but there was no one to help. . . . "*

41. St. Peter Gallicantu

*"Remember that Satan has asked for you,
to sift you all like wheat" (Luke 22:31).*

My visit to the Church of St. Peter Gallicantu was something special because I love St. Peter. The name of the church is interesting. Gallicantu means "cockcrow." Jesus warned Peter, "I give you my word, before the cock crows tonight you will deny me three times" (*Matthew 26:34*). This Scripture passage could have one of two meanings: Jesus might have meant before the early morning rooster announces the dawn of a new day, or He might have been referring to that time of morning when the guard was changed, which was also called the cockcrow.

Supposedly this is the place where the palace of the high priest, Caiaphas, stood and to which Jesus was brought for the first part of that mock trial. Peter came to warm himself at the fire in the courtyard and was there accused of being one of Jesus' followers. This came as a terrible threat to Peter, who rashly and thoughtlessly denied that he even knew Jesus.

A little later, as the temple guard dragged Jesus from the palace of the high priest, "The Lord turned around and looked at Peter, and Peter remembered the word that the Lord had spoken to

141

him, 'Before the cock crows today you will deny me three times.' He went out and wept bitterly" (*Luke 22:61*).

On this beautiful property overlooking the Kidron Valley the Assumptionist Fathers have built a new church. Excavations have revealed a paved street which leads from the Cenacle to the Pool of Siloam. This street was probably traversed by Jesus on the first Holy Thursday evening.

Under the church there is a large grotto which is venerated as the dungeon in which Jesus was held prisoner the night before He was taken to the praetorium for Pilate's confirmation of His death sentence. Another grotto beneath the church is held sacred and is believed to be the room in which Peter found refuge immediately after his denial and where he wept bitterly.

There is some question as to whether or not this was the exact location of the palace of the high priest. On the other hand, we know from the Gospel account that the event did take place. This is the only aspect with which we are concerned in our life of prayer. We leave the scientific aspect to be dealt with by the scholars.

We had the privilege of returning to St. Peter Gallicantu for our Easter Vigil Liturgy. We were joined by other English-speaking groups. This Paschal Liturgy of rejoicing and commitment was an ideal preparation for the glorious Feast of the Resurrection.

I appreciated this spot because I love St. Peter. He was impetuous, blundering, brash, but always humble, docile, lovable and loving. I can identify with all of Peter's weaknesses. I recognize myself so frequently in his failings. On the other hand, while I cannot identify with his virtues, they do challenge me.

This incident of Peter's denial reveals much to us

about the person of Jesus. He did not reject Peter nor did He give up hope for him. He simply looked at Peter with unspeakable love and forgiveness. That sorrowful gaze of Jesus had power in it. Peter came to repentance. He became a New Man, a man who loved Jesus with all the more intensity. Love is born of repentance. Such repentance is willing to suffer anything for the person loved. Peter later proved this when he was crucified upside down.

May the Lord's Word to us carry with it that look of loving forgiveness, and may His Word motivate us to the extremes to which only love can carry us.

Matthew 26:31-35 — *". . . before the cock crows tonight you will deny me three times."*

Matthew 10:16-42 — *"Whoever disowns me before men I will disown before my Father in heaven."*

Luke 22:54-62 — *"Woman, I do not know him."*

John 13:36-38 — *"I will lay down my life for you!"*

II Timothy 2:1-13 — *"But if we deny him he will deny us."*

John 21:15-19 — *"Simon, son of John, do you love me? . . . You know well that I love you."*

Psalm 34:1-23 — *"Glorify the Lord with me, let us together extol his name."*

42. Arch of the Ecce Homo

"There is no limit to love's forbearance . . . "
(I Corinthians 13:7).

Our first stop on the way to Via Dolorosa was the Basilica of the Ecce Homo. As we approached the basilica we could see a portion of a large arch spanning the street and disappearing into the wall of the basilica. Later we discovered that the other portion of this arch enframes the altar in the main chapel.

The Sisters of Sion welcomed us very warmly here. These Sisters have a specialized apostolate of establishing, maintaining and deepening Judaeo-Christian relations. They were founded in the nineteenth century by a Jewish convert for this precise work. Today the Sisters operate a large hospice here, where they welcome pilgrims, furnish them with valuable information about Jerusalem and the Holy Land, and at times guide them to these sacred places.

We first went to the Lithostrotos (stone pavement), or in Aramaic, Gabbatha (raised place). This is the traditional site where Jesus was mocked and ridiculed as king. The area is covered with large flagstones. These stones were striated with very close grooves which prevented horses from slipping. Here and there canals hollowed out in the stones catch rainwater and conduct it to a subterranean cistern. This cistern is still being used as a water supply.

On some of the large flagstones are incised games which the soldiers played. They were much like our hopscotch, maze, etc. One of these games,

A Friday procession on the Via Dolorosa, the path taken by Jesus on His way to Calvary.

very popular in the Roman army, was called "the game of the king." This game consisted chiefly of choosing a burlesque king, who was ridiculed, mocked and loaded with all sorts of ludicrous honors, and then put to death at the end of the farce. It seems evident from the Gospels that the soldiers played this game with Jesus. "They stripped off his clothes and wrapped him in a scarlet military cloak. Weaving a crown out of thorns they fixed it on his head, and stuck a reed in his right hand" (*Matthew 27:28ff*).

Here in the Lithostrotos, which is now incorporated into the building, we had the privilege of offering the Holy Sacrifice of the Mass on a portable altar next to one of these flagstones with a game incised in it. During the Mass my eyes kept returning to the stone. I could almost hear the scorning derision of the pagan Roman soldiers who hated the Jews with a vengeance. I could almost visualize the humble, long-suffering, patient God of heaven and earth as the object of their cruel, diabolical glee.

On our return to Jerusalem for Holy Week, we had the great privilege of returning to the Lithostrotos for the Good Friday Liturgy. I shall long remember this Liturgy in the very spot where Jesus accepted ignominy for my sins. It was raining outside and the noise of the rain beating on the pavement spoke to me of the tears that the angels must have shed at this miscarriage of justice and the vicious hatred which initiated it. The thought which kept recurring to me: "I did it for you, too."

St. Ignatius in his *Spiritual Exercises* outlines what he is pleased to call the three kinds of humility. He defines the third kind of humility in these words: "Whenever the praise and glory of the Divine Majesty would be equally served, in order to imitate and be in reality more like Christ, our

Lord, I desire and choose poverty with Christ poor, rather than riches; insults with Christ loaded with them, rather than honors; I desire to be accounted as worthless and a fool for Christ, rather than to be esteemed as wise and prudent in this world. So Christ was treated before me" (#167, *Spiritual Exercises*).

May our praying with His Word help us to form this attitude more completely in our daily living.

Psalm 22:6-9 — *"But I am a worm, not a man; the scorn of men, despised by the people."*

Isaiah 52:13-15; 53:1-12 — *" . . . many were amazed at him — so marred was his look beyond that of man. . . . "*

Matthew 26:57-68 — *"Play the prophet for us, Messiah!"*

Matthew 27:11-31 — *"Then they began to mock him . . . 'All hail, king of the Jews!' "*

John 18:28-40 — *"If he were not a criminal . . . we would certainly not have handed him over to you."*

John 19:1-15 — *"Pilate said to them, 'Look at the man!' "*

James 1:12-15 — *"Happy the man who holds out to the end through trial!"*

43. The Praetorium

". . . by his stripes we were healed"
(Isaiah 53:5).

I found several chapels built on and around the Franciscan compound close to St. Stephen's Gate, or the Lion's Gate as it is sometimes called. To the right as you enter the compound is the Chapel of Flagellation, which supposedly marks the site where Jesus suffered inhuman scourging. In this chapel three stained glass windows recall the dreadful scene which took place here in this barracks yard: the Flagellation, Pilate Washing His Hands, and the Triumph of Barabbas. An altar in honor of St. Paul, the Apostle of the Gentiles, is found as soon as one enters the chapel. The altar is a reminder that St. Paul, like his Master, was a prisoner in this fortress.

Another chapel, to the left as one enters the compound, is called the Chapel of Condemnation and of the Imposition of the Cross. This chapel is located at the end of the Lithostrotos on which Pilate stood when he publicly condemned Jesus to death. Here also Jesus accepted His cross.

Nearby is Al' Omariyeh College. This building, situated on a great rock overlooking the Temple, is part of the fortress which the Roman garrison used.

We entered the courtyard by walking up a ramp to the site of the Praetorium. The Via Dolorosa usually begins here in this courtyard.

The Jewish leaders already had sentenced Jesus to death, but their verdict had to be ratified by the Roman Governor. Very early in the morning on that first Good Friday, they brought Jesus to Pontius Pilate and demanded the death penalty. Part of the mock trial of Jesus was held in the private palace which the Jewish leaders did not enter because they did not want to be defiled. "They did not enter the praetorium themselves, for they had to avoid ritual impurity if they were to eat the Passover" (*John 18:28*). The public part of that farcical trial took place on the Lithostrotos, where the mob screamed: "Crucify him! Crucify him!"

It took some time for me to put all this together. At first I found it difficult to pinpoint all the geographic areas where Jesus, the eternal, almighty Son of God, suffered such inhuman treatment at the hands of His creatures. At last I concluded that the exact location was unimportant.

I then began to experience another emotion. I felt bitterness, resentment and anger welling up in me as I reflected how Jesus had been degraded, derided, blasphemed — how He had been treated as a fool, a buffoon for the sport of these men. I was furious when I thought of the agonizing pain He had endured at the cruel scourging. Here I wanted to cry out, "How could people have done such a thing?"

These feelings were only momentary, thanks be to God. I realized that Jesus is alive, that He is gloriously reigning and living with me and within me. How, then, would the Risen Jesus want me to react?

I am sure that Jesus would want me to sit at His side while we would review, not in any masochistic way, all that He had suffered. He would remind me that He suffered such inhuman treatment because He loves us. He would remind me that because of His infinite love, He went far beyond what was asked of Him. He emptied Himself totally and completely to prove that genuine love knows no bounds. Jesus would remind me that the Evangelist John always spoke of His sufferings as His glorification.

I sat for a long time in the warm spring sunshine that afternoon. As I pondered these events with the Risen Jesus within me, I experienced a deep sense of gratitude and appreciation for His great love. I found myself responding to His love with a greater intensity. My heart was filled with compassion as I was moved to say to Jesus that I would be willing to accept whatever pain, rejection, ridicule or suffering He was pleased to ask of me, so long as His Kingdom would be served by it.

As you listen to His Word, may you be inflamed with love in response to His love.

Job 19:2-29 — *"Pity me, pity me, O you my friends, for the hand of God has struck me!"*

Psalm 118:19-29 — *"The stone which the builders rejected has become the cornerstone."*

Isaiah 52:13-53:12 — *"He was spurned and avoided by men, a man of suffering, . . . and we held him in no esteem."*

Amos 2:4-5 — *". . . they spurned the law of the Lord. . . . "*

Luke 10:1-20 — *"He who hears you, hears me. He who rejects you, rejects me."*

Luke 17:22-37 — *"The Son of Man . . . must suffer much and be rejected. . . . "*

I Peter 2:4-10 — *"Come to him, a living stone, rejected by men but approved, nonetheless. . . . "*

44. Jesus Meets His Mother

*"His burden shall be taken
from your shoulder . . . " (Isaiah 10:27).*

As we passed under the Arch of the Ecce Homo,
we came to what is venerated as the site of the first
fall of Jesus under His cross. We made our way
through the crowds of people living in the Old
City. They were buying their daily supply of bread
and produce. The shopkeepers pleaded with us to
patronize their wares. Little donkeys were busy
carrying huge loads of vegetables on their backs to
various shops for resale. All this added to, rather
than detracted from, my reflection at this location.

The Gospel does not mention the first fall of
Jesus commemorated by the Third Station, but tradition finds tacit approval in the Gospel which nar-
rates how the soldiers forced Simon of Cyrene to
carry the cross with Jesus. Until a few years ago
the Third Station was marked by a column lying
on the ground. Today that column serves as a pillar
for the iron railing in front of the little chapel. A
high relief depicts the fall of Jesus.

A few yards beyond is the Armenian Catholic
Church. The door on the left indicates the site of
the Fourth Station, where Jesus and Mary met. In
the excavation of this church a mosaic was found,
picturing two feet pointing northwest. Today a
person is reminded of this Station by a half-bust of
Jesus with His Mother displayed on the wall of a
small oratory. Within the church an altar represents
Jesus meeting His Mother.

A short distance from the church, the street
turns uphill to Calvary. Here the first building on
the left is an oratory marking the Fifth Station,
where the Roman legionaries forced Simon, who
was coming in from the fields, to carry the cross of

Jesus. This compulsory service for Jesus sufficed to preserve the name of Simon down through the ages.

The trafficking was so heavy that I found a little niche in which I could stand and reflect on what took place here. There is a tradition that all three events took place at one spot. Jesus was exhausted from the Agony in Gethsemane, having spent the whole night in torturous suffering. The scourging, crowning with thorns, and great loss of blood had all so weakened Jesus that He was unable to carry this heavy instrument of His death. As I pondered these scenes it all made sense.

When Jesus fell beneath His cross, His Mother undoubtedly rushed forward to comfort her Son amid the insults and taunts of the executioners, His accusers and the rabble close behind. The executioners could readily see that Jesus was not strong enough to reach the hill of Calvary; hence they immediately found Simon of Cyrene to carry the cross with Jesus.

A new image now came to mind. As I stood in that niche with the ebb and flow of the crowd brushing by me, I realized that I was not alone. Together with the Risen Jesus living within me, we were recalling what took place here. I found great encouragement in my reflection. The Lord seemed to be telling me that when He asks us to accept and bear a cross, we are never alone. When the cross seems heavy and impossible and we are apt to fall beneath it, then we have the assurance that His Mother will always be there to comfort and assist us. Jesus had already taught us how pleasing is His Mother's powerful intercession (*John 2*). Furthermore, Jesus founded His Church as a community, a family. He will always send someone to support, encourage and assist us when the cross becomes too heavy. We know that we will always find sympathetic support from our brothers and sisters in Christ.

Frequently we need to recall His loving providential care and concern for us. It is so easy to become oblivious to this in our hectic day-to-day living. These suggested scriptural readings will help to renew that conviction.

Isaiah 11:1-9 — "Justice shall be the band around his waist, and faithfulness a belt upon his hips."

Matthew 27:32-34 — "On their way out they met a Cyrenian named Simon. This man they pressed into service to carry the Cross."

Luke 2:22-35 — "This child is destined to be the downfall and the rise of many. . . . "

Luke 23:26-31 — "Daughters of Jerusalem, do not weep for me. Weep for yourselves and for your children."

John 19:16-18 — "Jesus was led away, . . . carrying the cross by himself. . . . "

Romans 11:11-24 — " . . . does their stumbling mean that they are forever fallen?"

I Corinthians 10:1-13 — " . . . let anyone who thinks he is standing upright watch out lest he fall!"

45. Veronica

"May the Lord reward what you have done!"
(Ruth 2:12).

Another favorite place of mine along the Via Dolorosa is the Sixth Station. To the casual tourist this Station is marked by an archway over the street and a fragment of a column inserted in the wall, but there is much more to it than first meets the eye. A door in the wall of stone opens to a stairway leading to the Church of St. Veronica. This is the traditional site of the house of the noble woman who came forward with a linen cloth soaked in cold water which she raised to the face of Jesus covered with dirt, blood and spittle. Jesus rewarded this courageous act of love by returning the cloth to her with the features of His sacred face imprinted upon it.

Tradition relates that this woman was the same woman who had suffered for 12 years with the issue of blood and whom Jesus had cured as she touched His garment. In gratitude this woman followed Jesus wherever He went. Tradition has also named this woman Veronica. However, the name probably developed from the description of what took place at this Station. The name comes from "vera icone," which means "true image."

The Church of St. Veronica is a simple, plain chapel. Under the church some ancient vaults were turned into an oratory. This place is cared for by the Little Sisters of Jesus. Following Brother Charles de Foucauld, the Little Sisters of Jesus are essentially contemplatives, bringing a presence of prayer and friendship especially in those areas where they do manual work to support themselves. They earn their living in the same way as their neighbors, taking factory jobs in cities, doing handcraft work along with other craftsmen, or sharing the life of farm workers.

These Sisters were most gracious and kind to us. They spoke very seldom and only when necessary, but the peace that radiated from their smiling faces spoke eloquently.

I went back to the oratory often to spend time in prayer. This oratory is a vault made of stone, with a stone altar and stone seats along the sides. It is a devotional spot for prayer. The small semicircular stained glass windows face a narrow passageway outside which may be called a street. It is a busy road with people, donkeys and sheep all weaving, bobbing and pushing their way through the crowds. The noise and confusion of the street filtered into the chapel, but it was not distracting. It was rather like background music to my prayer. I am sure that the same noise and jostling was heard and felt by Jesus as He made His way up and down this street many times. There is no doubt that as He was making His way up this street on the way to His execution, the same noise rang in His ears along with the greater crescendo of insults and abuse which was being leveled upon Him by His enemies.

I was drawn back to this chapel many times during our sojourn in Jerusalem. For me, it was so easy to pray here in this austere oratory.

I prayed here for all the Veronicas I know, for all those wonderful Veronicas who may not bear the name but who, like Veronica, are ministering to the Body of Jesus all over the world, whether it be to their own family, their neighbors or those casual acquaintances whom the Lord sends into their lives. I prayed that they may always and everywhere reflect the image of Jesus to all who cross their path.

I thanked God also for the gift of Veronica and

her noble, heroic act of love. I had to ask myself if I am eager to reach out with the same manifestation of love to others in need. Am I sufficiently courageous to reach out in love to a person surrounded by enemies who are assassinating his character, robbing him of his rights, ridiculing him as a person? I prayed earnestly for that degree of love.

May we find inspiration, encouragement and motivation from these exemplars of love whom God has raised up for our edification and emulation.

Luke 8:43-48 — *"Daughter, it is your faith that has cured you. Now go in peace."*

Esther 4:14-30 — *"Help me, who am alone and have no help but you, for I am taking my life in my hand."*

Psalm 31:2-25 — *". . . they who see me abroad flee from me. . . . I hear the whispers of the crowd, that frighten me from every side. . . . "*

Judith 13:17-20 — *"Your deed of hope will never be forgotten by those who tell of the might of God."*

Isaiah 25:1-12 — *"The Lord God will wipe away the tears from all faces. . . . "*

Psalm 51:2-21 — *". . . wash me, and I shall be whiter than snow."*

II Maccabees 7:20-29 — *"Do not be afraid of this executioner, but be worthy of your brothers and accept death, so that in the time of mercy I may receive you again with them."*

Place of the Skull — Golgotha

". . . and I — once I am lifted up from earth —
will draw all men to myself"
(John 12:30).

My first visit to Calvary was a shocking disappointment, because my expectations were un-
realistic. My frequent reflections on the Gospel's
description of Calvary lingered in my mind. Some-
how I expected to see Calvary as it might have
appeared 2,000 years ago. Instead I was surprised
to find the gigantic Basilica of the Holy Sepulchre
built over the area of the last scenes of the Way of
the Cross. A person cannot see the whole rock, nor
the tomb, nor the place of the apparitions on Resurrection Day. The monumental edifices covering
these sacred spots were built over the years by the
piety of pilgrims. In addition to this momentary
shock, the basilica was crowded and confusion
seemed to reign everywhere.

I had come to pray, but that was impossible.
Instead, I made a complete tour of the basilica and
its many chapels, trying to reconstruct the places
where all the momentous events from Good Friday
through Easter Sunday had taken place.

I did learn that the basilica opens each morning
at 4:30. I came back the next morning to find
myself alone, with the exception of the two Sisters
who had come with me to pray.

As one enters the Church of the Holy Sepulchre,
one finds a stairway of 14 steps leading to the
Chapel of Golgotha. A part of the chapel is built
on the rock of Calvary. The chapel is divided down
the middle, without any line of demarcation. On
the right is the Latin Chapel and on the left, the
Greek Chapel.

In the Greek Chapel a marble altar stands over

the rock in which the Cross of Jesus was fixed. Under the altar, in the center, is a hole through which you can put your hand to touch the rock itself. The chapel on the right, which belongs to the Latin Church, is the site of the Thirteenth Station — the Stabat Mater — where Mary received Jesus into her arms.

I found a secluded corner. There was not a soul stirring. Silence reigned, but it was not a dead silence. Here in the dim light of early morning great shadows blotted out the blemishes of time. It became easier to visualize these sacred sites and to contemplate what had taken place here. The descriptions which the Evangelists give help us to relive the last hours of Jesus on earth.

As I prayed, nestled in a little corner, my reflection naturally turned to our compassionate Father who loved us so much that He gave us His own Son to pay the penalty of our sins and to span the breach which sin had caused. Jesus did not have to go to this extreme, but He experienced the infinite love of the Father and His response to that love would know no bounds. He wanted to give everything, and He did.

As I pondered that forgiving, healing and redeeming love of Jesus, I realized how personal Jesus had made that love in the Sacrament of Reconciliation. Jesus wanted to pour out that forgiving, healing and redeeming love upon each one of us personally and individually. He does just that in an extraordinary way each time we meet Him in the Sacrament of Reconciliation.

I wanted to meet Jesus in this Sacrament of peace and pardon right here on the top of Calvary where He poured out His last drop of blood for me. Even though there was no priest in evidence, I began to prepare myself anyway. Sometime later, as I looked up, I saw the brown robe of a Franciscan priest approaching in the shadows. He not only spoke English, but he was also delighted to administer the Sacrament of Reconciliation. Meeting Jesus here in His compassionate sacramental presence meant very much to me.

God had another surprise for me. The two Sisters who had accompanied me approached to ask if they might also receive the Sacrament. On this morning, right here on Calvary's Hill, my priestly role as the sacramental dispenser of His forgiving, healing and redeeming love became much more significant to me than ever before. With tear-filled eyes I breathed a fervent, "Thank You, Lord!"

As we spend time with Jesus in prayer, His forgiving, healing, redeeming love will become more real to us.

John 19:16-37 — "Jesus was led away . . . to what is called the Place of the Skull (in Hebrew, Golgotha)."

Luke 23:33-49 — "Father, forgive them; they do not know what they are doing."

Psalm 22:1-32 — "My God, my God, why have you forsaken me? . . . "

Matthew 27:33-55 — "From noon onward, there was darkness over the whole land. . . . "

Habakkuk 3:1-19 — " . . . his look makes the nations tremble. The eternal mountains are shattered. . . . "

Mark 15:21-32 — "Save yourself now by coming down from that cross!"

*Isaiah 54:1-17 — "Though . . . the hills be shaken,
My love shall never leave you. . . . "*

47. Resurrection

*"Destroy this temple, . . . and in three days
I will raise it up" (John 2:19).*

Easter Sunday in Jerusalem! What a dream! I
spent Easter morning in the Chapel of the Little
Sisters of Jesus along the Via Dolorosa. This chapel
is a vault under the Church of St. Veronica. Its
walls, floor and ceiling are all hewn out of rock. I
wanted to be here because it resembles in so many
aspects the tomb from which Jesus came forth in
all His glory. I wanted to be in this vaulted chapel
because on previous visits I always found it prayerful. The contemplative atmosphere which the
Little Sisters of Jesus bring here permeates the
whole locale. I had the privilege of spending several
hours here with the Easter Alleluias, with all the
stops pulled, ringing in my heart.

In the afternoon we went to the Basilica of the
Holy Sepulchre. Our first stop was the Chapel of
the Apparition of Jesus. St. John tells us in his
Gospel that there was a garden close by the place
where Jesus was executed. It was in this garden
that Jesus was laid in the tomb by Joseph of Ari-
mathaea and Nicodemus. It was in this same garden
that Mary Magdalene wandered, bewildered and
distraught, because the body of Jesus was not in
the tomb as she had expected. It was here that she

recognized Jesus by the sound of His voice when He called her by name. As I reflected on this event, I thought of the Lord calling me also by name. Did He not say, "I have called you by name: you are mine" (*Isaiah 43:1*)?

We were fortunate to be able to celebrate our Easter Mass in the Latin Chapel, which is called the Chapel of the Apparition of Jesus to His Mother. The Gospel does not speak of this appearance of Jesus to His Mother, but a longstanding tradition in the Church perpetuates its probability. I like to think that Jesus really did visit His Mother first after His Resurrection. I support this tradition even though it is not mentioned in the Gospel account.

This chapel is under the care of the Franciscan Fathers. They received us warmly and prepared everything for our glorious Eucharistic Celebration on this Easter Sunday. We joined them in singing the Holy Office and then celebrated our own Easter Mass.

In this beautiful chapel we also saw the pillar to which Jesus was tied for the scourging. It is placed on an altar at the right side of the chapel. This pillar is called the "Column of the Flagellation." It is a fragment of a porphyry column about three feet high.

Our Easter Mass was a joyous occasion as we sang with gusto the Alleluias along with other appropriate hymns. I thought of what hope and promise the events which took place at this site brought to the entire world. The whole Paschal Mystery was enacted in this very area and spread from here to every corner of the world.

This Paschal Mystery is made available to us at each Holy Mass. The same Risen Jesus celebrates with us. Even more, that same Risen Jesus is living within each one of us. That is what His Resurrection is all about.

Our time in prayer will deepen this conviction and keep the joy of Easter ever alive in our hearts.

Matthew 28:1-15 — *". . . he is not here. He has been raised, exactly as he promised."*

Luke 24:1-13 — *"Why do you search for the Living One among the dead?"*

Romans 6:1-23 — *"If we have been united with him through likeness to his death, so shall we be through a like resurrection."*

II Maccabees 7:1-41 — *". . . the King of the world will raise us up to live again forever."*

John 20:1-18 — *"Early in the morning . . . Mary Magdalene came to the tomb."*

I Corinthians 15:1-28 — *"Just as in Adam all die, so in Christ all will come to life again. . . ."*

Psalm 118:1-29 — *"This is the day the Lord has made; let us be glad and rejoice in it."*

48. Easter at the Cenacle

"Peace be with you . . . " (John 20:19).

Another hallowed place to celebrate Easter is in the Cenacle. As it stands today the Cenacle has several rooms on different levels. One of the first-floor rooms is pointed out as the room in which the disciples were assembled behind closed doors "for fear of the Jews."

On the day of the Resurrection Jesus came in all His glory to announce to them that He was really alive and risen from the dead as He had promised. On so many previous occasions He tried to explain His Resurrection to them, but they could not comprehend what He was saying.

The apparitions of Jesus on Resurrection Day served many purposes. He appeared to bring comfort, hope and reassurance to all His friends who suffered along with Him. He also showed Himself alive to dispel any doubt or misgivings about His Resurrection. What joy and peace this brought to all those hearts who loved Him deeply!

On Easter Sunday I was not able to spend time in this room of the Apparition in the Cenacle, but my previous visits there had done much for me. As I sat in this room and reflected on the great mystery of God's love, my heart was filled with a joy and peace which cannot easily be verbalized.

It was in this very room that Jesus instituted that marvelous Sacrament of Reconciliation. He commissioned His apostles to go forth and bring forgiveness, healing and redemption to others. Jesus told them that as the Father had sent Him, He was now sending them to carry on His mission of healing and forgiveness. He imparted to them the same power which the Father had given Him. "Receive the Holy Spirit. If you forgive men's sins, they are forgiven them" (*John 20:22-23*).

It is true that by His passion and death Jesus did make reparation for all our sins, but now He wanted to establish a viable means whereby that loving forgiveness and healing could be channeled to us individually. Through the Sacrament of Reconciliation Jesus made His forgiveness and healing more personal.

The Father loves us so much that He sent His only Son to redeem us, but this redemptive act could seem to us quite general and universal. We need a more personal assurance of His loving forgiveness. In the Sacrament of Reconciliation we encounter Jesus personally as He comes to assure us individually that He is forgiving and healing us. How gracious of Jesus to take each one of us into consideration! How infinite His compassion, which channels His loving forgiveness and healing to each one of us! What a blessing this Sacrament is! What reassurance! What peace and joy He brings us!

A deeper joy and peace came to me as I sat possibly in the very room in which Jesus instituted this Sacrament of Reconciliation. The Cenacle was the place where at least three Sacraments were instituted: the Eucharist, the Priesthood and what is now called the Sacrament of Reconciliation.

As we reflect on His loving kindness to us, should we not ask for a deeper appreciation of this Sacrament? Our gratitude can best be shown by receiving the Sacrament often and well, as Jesus intended. May our hearts overflow with peace and joy because of His sacramental forgiveness and healing.

Mark 16:1-8 — "He has been raised up; he is not here."

John 20:19-29 — "If you forgive men's sins, they are forgiven. . . . "

Matthew 28:16-20 — "Teach them to carry out everything I have commanded you."

Acts 10:34-43 — " . . . only to have God raise him up on the third day . . . "

Colossians 3:1-17 — "Be intent on things above rather than on things of earth."

I Peter 1:3-12 — " . . . he who in his great mercy gave us a new birth . . . "

I Corinthians 15:29-58 — "Death is swallowed up in victory."

49. Emmaus

" . . . he was revealed to them completely changed in appearance" (Mark 16:12).

One of my favorite episodes in the Gospel narrative is the account of the two disciples on their way to Emmaus on the first Easter Sunday. We went to Emmaus on Easter Monday. We would have liked to retrace the way the disciples walked, but time and energy did not permit a seven-mile walk. Instead we travelled by bus on a circuitous route. It was a gorgeous day. We spent our travelling time singing and silently reflecting on the events that occurred on the road to Emmaus.

The present name for Emmaus is El Quebeieh, which means "little dome." A large church commemorates the site where the disciples invited Jesus to stay with them. The remains of the house of Cleopas can still be seen in the left nave of the church. The heavy walls rise above ground level and can be clearly seen as a house. This home is enclosed in the old church, which proves that it was venerated from the earliest Christian times.

Easter Monday is an important day and Emmaus is an important place for the Christian Arabs. We chose this day for our visit to Emmaus also. When we arrived, there was a gay and festive mood already prevailing. The Arabs celebrate this day with a Eucharistic Liturgy with the Bishop as principal celebrant. A day of jubilation complete with bands and dancing follows.

We celebrated the Eucharist with our own group privately in a beautiful garden next to the church. It was a joyous experience for all of us, just as the first Emmaus revelation must have been, not only for the two disciples, but for the whole Christian community. Recall that the disciples returned to Jerusalem immediately to share the Good News with the other followers of Jesus. Here at Emmaus Jesus came to us in the breaking of the bread, just as He had for these disciples. It was a real source of joy for us, too.

I find in the events of Emmaus many practical lessons for our own day-to-day living. In the first place, we are assured that the Risen Jesus is always with us and living within us wherever we go. Like the disciples we do not always recognize Him immediately in the happenings of each day. Mark says it so well: "He was revealed to them completely changed in appearance" (*Mark 16:12*). He may come into our lives completely changed and not as we expect to find Him. Nevertheless, we know that He is always with us and within us.

Secondly, Jesus opened up the Scriptures for the disciples and gave them such an understanding of the Word that their hearts were burning inside them. Jesus is always present in His Word and He speaks to us through the Word if we listen. Jesus answered the questions of the disciples and dispelled all their doubts by opening the Scriptures to them. He does the same for us today by showing us that suffering was necessary in His life and also in ours. The marvelous things which suffering can effect in our lives surpass all comprehension.

Thirdly, the disciples recognized Jesus in the breaking of the bread. Jesus did not force Himself upon the disciples. It was only after they invited Him to stay with them that He revealed Himself to them. "They pressed him: 'Stay with us.'" He does not force His way into our lives, but waits patiently for our invitation. We, too, will find Jesus dwelling among us, especially as we recognize Him in the Holy Eucharist.

Luke 24:13-35 — "... they had come to know him in the breaking of bread."

Proverbs 9:1-12 — "Instruct a wise man, and he becomes still wiser...."

Mark 16:9-20 — "... he was revealed to them completely changed in appearance."

Isaiah 2:1-5 — "Come, let us climb the Lord's Mountain, ... That he may instruct us in his ways...."

Matthew 10:1-20 — "The gift you have received, give as a gift."

Psalm 25:1-22 — "He guides the humble to justice, he teaches the humble his way."

I John 1:5-10 — "But if we walk in light, as he is in the light, we have fellowship with one another. . . . "

50. Church of the Primacy — Peter the Shepherd

"I will entrust to you the Keys of the kingdom of heaven" (Matthew 16:19).

A very special place for me along the Sea of Galilee was the spot where Jesus appeared to His apostles after the Resurrection. Here on the shore of this gorgeous lake Jesus prepared a breakfast for His fishermen friends after they miraculously caught 153 fish at His bidding.

A modest little chapel, called the Church of the Primacy, marks the site where Jesus stood. It is also called the "Place of the Coals," since Jesus had a "charcoal fire there with a fish laid on it and some bread" (*John 21:9*).

Here on this rocky shore Jesus made Peter the head of His Church. This place is sacred because here Jesus conferred the Primacy on St. Peter. After Peter's profession of faith at Banias, or in biblical terms Caesarea Philippi, Jesus promised that He would give him the keys to His Kingdom. After the Resurrection, when the mission of Jesus on earth was drawing to a close, He conferred on

Peter jurisdiction over the whole Church. Thus Jesus established a visible vicar on earth for our guidance and direction.

Here on the water's edge were built 12 thrones for the 12 apostles. Some of the ruins of these thrones can still be seen as the water of the lake laps around them. They are large heart-shaped stones which symbolize the love upon which the Kingdom of God is built.

The church built over the site is a small, modest church. I loved every square inch of it. It is a simple stone church with a plank floor and without furniture. Between the nave of the church and the altar a large, flat rock protrudes. This rock is called the Mensa Christi, the Table of Christ. This apparently is the rock on which Jesus served breakfast to His apostles after their unproductive night of fishing. When they drew up their boats on the shore, Jesus invited them to have something to eat. "Come and eat your meal," He said. It was after this meal that Jesus asked Peter three separate times if he loved Him.

We were able to pray here on the shore in balmy, spring morning weather. The gentle waves washing the rocky beach and the slight breeze wafting the fragrance of spring blooms served to enhance prayer. In my imagination I could almost see Jesus standing on one of the huge stones — perhaps taking a long stride or even a leap from one stone to another as He called out to His apostles, "Cast your net off the starboard side."

Later we concelebrated the Eucharistic Liturgy. It was a very moving celebration. The readings chosen for the Liturgy of the Word made present to us what took place here so long ago.

After Holy Communion one of our accomplished priest-vocalists sang Carey Landry's "Peter, Do You Really Love Me?" I do not think that we were a sentimental group, but I am sure that there was hardly a dry eye in that cozy little church that morning.

In my reflective prayer, I was deeply grateful for all that God had done for me. Here He established His Church, to which He invited me at the moment of my Baptism. At that moment I became a son of God and an heir of heaven. At that moment I also became a temple of the Holy Spirit, who pours out His divine love and life upon me.

Even more, He called me into His priesthood to minister under the leadership and direction of His visible vicar on earth, who is the successor of St. Peter and who can claim spiritual lineage from this very spot.

It is not surprising that in 1964 Pope Paul VI visited this spot to pray here for the entire Church. He also blessed the first stone for the new Shrine of the Primacy of Peter.

As you pray these Scriptures may your gratitude and faith be deepened and renewed.

Luke 9:18-22 — "But you — who do you say I am?"

John 21:1-14 — "Children, have you caught anything to eat?"

John 21:15-19 — "Simon, son of John, do you love me?"

Mark 14:27-31 — "Even though all are shaken in faith, it will not be that way with me."

II Peter 1:12-19 — "... we possess the prophetic message as something altogether reliable."

Galatians 2:1-10 — "... I had been entrusted with the gospel for the uncircumcised, just as Peter was for the circumcised. ..."

Acts 5:12-16 — "... when Peter passed by at least his shadow might fall on one or another of them."

51. The Dome of the Ascension

"I am ascending to my Father and your Father, to my God and your God!" (John 20:17).

Once again we were climbing the Mount of Olives. This time our destination was the Dome of the Ascension. It was a brilliant, warm spring morning. I observed that a quiet spirit of devotion and recollection prevailed in our small group as we walked along.

When we reached the summit a striking, and somewhat strange, panoramic view lay before us. On the east side the sandy Desert of Judaea sloped down into the Jordan Valley. It was framed by the bluish mountains of Gilead and Moab. In the valley we could also see the glassy surface of the Dead Sea. To our right lay the city of Jerusalem glittering in the bright morning sunshine. It is little wonder that this breathtaking sight filled the pilgrims with joy. Their joy found expression in the processional psalms which reverberated from their hearts as they journeyed toward the Holy City. Even though the Temple with all its glory is no more, the tangible presence of God seems to hover over this sacred site. With the psalmist I found myself praying: "Then will I go in to the altar of God, the God of my gladness and joy" (*Psalm 43:4*).

The spot of the Ascension is called Viri Galilaei — "Men of Galilee" — probably taken from Acts 1:11. We were told that the people of Galilee used to encamp here on this summit when they came to worship in the Temple. This may have had some influence on the name. Jesus probably spent many nights here as a boy when He came with Mary and Joseph to worship in the Temple for the big Feasts.

We entered the area through a big iron gate. Here we found a polygonal chapel with a cupola. It is a small shrine faced with two pillars. This shrine is built over a rock on which Jesus was supposed to have stood when He bade farewell to His apostles and ascended into heaven. The two columns are commemorative of the "two men dressed in white. . . . " " 'Men of Galilee,' they said, 'why do you stand here looking up at the skies?' " (*Acts 1:10*). As early as A.D. 380 the Church of the Ascension was built here to commemorate this hallowed spot.

As was our custom we visited the shrine, touched the stone on which Jesus was supposed to have stood, then found a quiet spot to spend some time in prayerful reflection.

The Ascension of Jesus into heaven is much more than this single scene of His departure on the Mount of Olives. The time, place and manner of Jesus' leaving His apostles after the final manifestation of Himself to them is relatively unimportant when we think of the mystery contained herein — a mystery which transcends the historical implications of the departure of Jesus.

Jesus was glorified through His Resurrection and now sits at the right hand of the Father. There are ample texts in Sacred Scripture which treat the celestial exaltation of Jesus where He is enthroned as King.

As I prayed at the Dome of the Ascension two reflections impressed themselves on my mind. In the first place Jesus commissioned each one of us to carry the message of the Good News to others and to radiate His love by our very life-style. This was not the mission given to the apostles only (*Matthew 28:18-20*), but an apostolate which is intended for all of us.

The second reflection which stirred my heart was the realization that heaven is our true home where we will be caught up in the eternal embrace of our loving Abba. In spite of His departure, Jesus did not leave us orphans. He remains with us in this land of exile through the indwelling of the Holy Spirit. He will continue to implement this divine life in us until we have reached our final destiny. Paul advises us to "set your hearts on what pertains to higher realms where Christ is seated at God's right hand." He further advises us: "Be intent on things above rather than on things of earth" (*Colossians 3:1f*). Again Paul assures us: "Indeed, we know . . . we have a dwelling provided for us by God, a dwelling in the heavens, not made by human hands but to last forever" (*II Corinthians 5:1*).

What hope the Ascension of Jesus brings to us! It takes us from this vale of tears to the new world where Jesus reigns. Like the apostles we can return to our daily routine duties "filled with joy." May Jesus, speaking through His Word, bring you that same hope and joy which filled the apostles.

Luke 24:46-53 — *"As he blessed, he left them, and was taken up to heaven."*

Ephesians 4:1-16 — "Rather, let us profess the truth in love and grow to the full maturity of Christ the head."

Acts 1:1-11 — "... he was lifted up before their eyes in a cloud which took him from their sight."

Hebrews 10:5-18 — "But Jesus offered one sacrifice for sins and took his seat forever at the right hand of God. ..."

Colossians 3:1-4 — "... set your heart on what pertains to higher realms where Christ is seated at God's right hand."

Ephesians 2:1-10 — "... it is owing to his favor that salvation is yours through faith."

I Peter 3:18-22 — "He went to heaven and is at God's right hand, with angelic rulers and powers subjected to him."

52. The Cenacle and the Holy Spirit

"The spirit of the Lord shall rest upon him . . ." (Isaiah 11:2).

I was anxious to return to the Cenacle to spend some time in prayer. My destination was that part of the Cenacle which is pointed out as the room in which the apostles and the Holy Women were gathered in prayer when the Holy Spirit was poured out upon them. When I arrived I found it very quiet and deserted. The room in which this earthshaking event took place is next to the room in which Jesus instituted the Sacraments of the Holy Eucharist and the Priesthood. Along the Eastern Wall there is a flight of eight steps leading down into a room in which is venerated the memory of the Descent of the Holy Spirit on Pentecost.

Before His Ascension into heaven, Jesus had instructed the apostles to "Remain here in the city until you are clothed with power from on high" (*Luke 24:49*). On another occasion " . . . he told them not to leave Jerusalem: 'Wait, rather, for the fulfillment of my Father's promise . . . ' " (*Acts 1:4*).

The apostles did exactly as Jesus had instructed them: "Entering the city, they went to the upstairs room where they were staying . . . " (*Acts 1:13*). The apostles spent the next 10 days in prayerful preparation for the coming of the Holy Spirit upon them. This was really a retreat. In prayer the apostles tried to make themselves receptive to whatever God was going to ask of them.

After 10 days of intense prayer, the Holy Spirit was poured out upon them. The strong driving wind, the tongues as of fire were external signs of the presence of the Holy Spirit. Luke's statement is brief, but powerful: "All were filled with the Holy Spirit."

I found an advantageous spot in this bare room and settled down on the floor with my back against the wall. It was a precious and peaceful time. The very atmosphere seemed to be permeated with a presence. I began to recall how the Holy Spirit was already operative in the prophets, judges and leaders in the Old Testament. The Christian era, too, was inaugurated by the Holy Spirit, who overshadowed Mary, filled Elizabeth, inspired Simeon and Anna, filled Zechariah, guided St. Joseph, and touched the hearts of many.

The Holy Spirit was operative in the life of Jesus. At His Baptism "the Spirit descended on him in visible form like a dove." And again, "Jesus full of the Holy Spirit, then returned from the Jordan and was conducted by the Spirit into the desert."

On the eve of His passion and death, Jesus told us very much about the work of the Holy Spirit in our lives. In that last discourse in the Upper Room, Jesus told us He would not leave us orphans, but would send the Holy Spirit to dwell with and within us, instruct us, convict us and be our source of truth.

Already, on Easter Sunday, Jesus asked for the outpouring of His Spirit upon the apostles in the Upper Room. The public manifestation of the Spirit took place on Pentecost. There were many Pentecosts which followed, as we find in the Acts of the Apostles.

I was remembering, too, that the Bishops in the Second Vatican Council reminded us of the tremendous influence of the Holy Spirit in our daily living.

As I basked in His presence with these encouraging thoughts crowding my mind, I prayed for a new and continued Pentecost in the lives of all of us. May His Word remind you of the power and presence of the Holy Spirit in your life.

Acts 2:1-13 — "All were filled with the Holy Spirit."

John 14:15-26 — *"I will ask the Father and he will give you another Paraclete — to be with you always. . . . "*

John 16:5-16 — *"When he comes, however, being the Spirit of truth he will guide you to all truth."*

Acts 10:34-48 — *"What can stop these people who have received the Holy Spirit, even as we have, from being baptized with water?"*

John 20:19-23 — *"Then he breathed on them and said: 'Receive the Holy Spirit.' "*

Galatians 5:13-26 — *"Since we live by the spirit, let us follow the spirit's lead."*

Acts 1:1-14 — *"You will receive power when the Holy Spirit comes down on you. . . . "*

DISCOVERING PATHWAYS TO PRAYER   1.75

By Msgr. David E. Rosage. Following Jesus was never meant to be dull, or worse, just duty-filled. Those who would aspire to a life of prayer and those who have already begun, will find this book amazingly thorough in its scripture-punctuated approach.

"A simple but profound book which explains the many ways and forms of prayer by which the person hungering for closer union with God may find him." **Emmanuel Spillane, O.C.S.O., Abbot, Our Lady of the Holy Trinity Abbey, Huntsville, Utah.**

THE BOOK OF REVELATION:
What Does It Really Say?   1.75

By Rev. John Randall S.T.D. The most discussed book of the Bible today is examined by a scripture expert in relation to much that has been published and the Truth. A simply written and revealing presentation.

THE ONE WHO LISTENS: A Book of Prayer   2.25

By Rev. Michael Hollings and Etta Gullick. Here the Spirit speaks through men and women of the past (St. John of the Cross, Thomas More, Dietrich Bonhoeffer), and present (Michel Quoist, Mother Teresa, Malcolm Boyd). There are also prayers from men of other faiths such as Muhammed and Tagore. God meets us where we are and since men share in sorrow, joy and anxiety, *their* prayers are *our* prayers. This is a book that will be outworn, perhaps, but never outgrown.

ENFOLDED BY CHRIST: An Encouragement to Pray 1.95

By Rev. Michael Hollings. This book helps us toward giving our lives to God in prayer yet at the same time remaining totally available to our fellowman — a difficult but possible feat. Father's sharing of his own difficulties and his personal approach convince us that "if he can do it, we can." We find in the author a true spiritual guardian and friend.

SOURCE OF LIFE:
The Eucharist and Christian Living   1.50

By Rev. Rene Voillaume. A powerful testimony to the vital part the
Eucharist plays in the life of a Christian. It is a product of a man for
whom Christ in the Euchartist is nothing less than all.

REASONS FOR REJOICING
Experiences in Christian Hope   1.75

Rev. Kenneth J. Zanca. God's love is a gift, not a reward. This
realization marks the beginning of mature faith and steeps our lives
in confidence and joy. In clear, non-pious, non-technical language,
Father Zanca offers a way to interpret the religious dimension in the
everyday experiences of being forgiven, seeking God, praying, celebrating and confronting suffering/evil.

*"It is a refreshing Christian approach to the Good News, always
emphasizing the love and mercy of God in our lives, and our response to that love in Christian hope."* **Brother Patrick Hart, Secre-
tary to the late Thomas Merton**

CONTEMPLATIVE PRAYER:
Problems and An Approach for the Ordinary Christian 1.75

Rev. Alan J. Placa. This inspiring book covers much ground: the
struggle of prayer, growth in familiarity with the Lord and the
sharing process. In addition, he clearly outlines a method of contemplative prayer for small groups based on the belief that private communion with God is essential to, and must precede, shared prayer.
The last chapter provides model prayers, taken from our Western
heritage, for the enrichment of private prayer experience.

CRISIS OF FAITH
Invitation to Christian Maturity   1.50

By Rev. Thomas Keating, ocso. How to hear ourselves called to
discipleship in the Gospels is Abbot Thomas' important and engrossing message. As Our Lord forms His disciples, and deals with His
friends or with those who come asking for help in the Gospels, we
can receive insights into the way He is forming or dealing with us in
our day to day lives.

PETALS OF PRAYER: Creative Ways To Pray

By Rev. Paul Sauvé   1.50

"Petals of Prayer *is an extremely practical book for anyone who desires to pray but has difficulty finding a method for so doing. At least 15 different methods of prayer are described and illustrated in simple, straightforward ways, showing they can be contemporary even though many of them enjoy a tradition of hundreds of years.* . . . Father Sauvé masterfully shows how traditional methods of prayer can be very much in tune with a renewed church."

St. Anthony Messenger

SEEKING PURITY OF HEART: THE GIFT OF OURSELVES TO GOD   illus 1.25

By Joseph Breault. For those of us who feel that we do not live up to God's calling, that we have sin of whatever shade within our hearts. This book shows how we can begin a journey which will lead from our personal darkness to wholeness in Christ's light — a purity of heart. Clear, practical help is given us in the constant struggle to free ourselves from the deceptions that sin has planted along all avenues of our lives.

IN GOD'S PROVIDENCE:
The Birth of a Catholic
Charismatic Parish   1.50

By Rev. John Randall. The engrossing story of the now well-known Word of God Prayer Community in St. Patrick's Parish, Providence, R.I. as it developed from Father Randall's first adverse reaction to the budding Charismatic Movement to today as it copes with the problems of being a truly pioneer Catholic Charismatic Parish.

"This splendid little volume bubbles over with joy and peace, with 'Spirit' and work."
The Priest

PROMPTED BY THE SPIRIT   2.25

By Rev. Paul Sauvé. A handbook by a Catholic Charismatic Renewal national leader for all seriously concerned about the future of the renewal and interested in finding answers to some of the problems that have surfaced in small or large prayer groups. It is a call to all Christians to find answers with the help of a wise Church tradition as transmitted by her ordained ministers. The author has also written *Petals of Prayer/Creative Ways to Pray.*

Books by Venard Polusney, O. Carm.

UNION WITH THE LORD IN PRAYER
Beyond Meditation To Affective Prayer Aspiration And Contemplation
.85

"A magnificent piece of work. It touches on all the essential points of Contemplative Prayer. Yet it brings such a sublime subject down to the level of comprehension of the 'man in the street,' and in such an encouraging way."
Abbott James Fox, O.C.S.O. (former superior of Thomas Merton at the Abbey of Gethsemani)

ATTAINING SPIRITUAL MATURITY FOR CONTEMPLATION (According to St. John of the Cross)
.85

"I heartily recommend this work with great joy that at last the sublime teachings of St. John of the Cross have been brought down to the understanding of the ordinary Christian without at the same time watering them down. For all (particularly for charismatic Christians) hungry for greater contemplation."
Rev. George A Maloney, S.J., Editor of Diakonia, Professor of Patristics and Spirituality, Fordham University.

THE PRAYER OF LOVE ... THE ART OF ASPIRATION
1.50

"It is the best book I have read which evokes the simple and loving response to remain in love with the Lover. To read it meditatively, to imbibe its message of love, is to have it touch your life and become part of what you are."
Mother Dorothy Guilbault, O. Carm., Superior General, Lacombe, La.

From the writings of John of St. Samson, O. Carm., mystic and charismatic

PRAYER, ASPIRATION AND CONTEMPLATION
Translated and edited by Venard Poslusney, O. Carm.   Paper 3.95

All who seek help in the exciting journey toward contemplation will find in these writings of John of St. Samson a compelling inspiration and support along with the practical guidance needed by those who travel the road of prayer.

LIVING FLAME PRESS
BOX 74
LOCUST VALLEY, N.Y. 11560

Order from your bookstore or use this coupon.

Please send me:

Quantity

_____	Praying With Scripture — $2.25
_____	Source of Life — $1.50
_____	The Book of Revelation — $1.75
_____	Reasons for Rejoicing — $1.75
_____	Discovering Pathways to Prayer — $1.75
_____	Prompted by the Spirit — $2.25
_____	Prayer of Love — $1.50
_____	Prayer, Aspiration & Contemplation — $3.95
_____	Union with the Lord — $.85
_____	Enfolded by Christ — $1.95
_____	Contemplative Prayer — $1.75
_____	Attaining Spiritual Maturity — $.85
_____	Petals of Prayer — $1.50
_____	Seeking Purity of Heart — $1.25
_____	Crisis of Faith — $1.50
_____	In God's Providence — $1.50
_____	The One Who Listens — $2.25

QUANTITY ORDER: DISCOUNT RATES

For convents, prayer groups, etc.: $10 to $25 = 10%;
$26 to $50 = 15%; over $50 = 20%.
Booksellers: 40%, 30 days net.

NAME_____

ADDRESS_____

CITY_____ STATE _____ ZIP _____

☐ *Payment enclosed. Kindly include $.35 postage and handling on
order up to $5.00. Above that, include 5% of total. Thank you.*